"The FASE method offers the tools to tackle the conscious and unconscious unbalanced in our day-to-day lives, both in terms of planning and prioritisation as well as mental and physical energy. The book delivers its side of the bargain: method, knowledge and clear rules that generate immediate returns. You deliver the other side: commitment, discipline and the willingness to do what it takes to improve."

POL CODINA,

VP Commercialitation Pepsico - Europe Region

"This book has been a guide to organising my day-to-day life. Its Simple and realistic "recipes" have helped me increase my productivity at work and have a sense of peace and organisation. All this is reflected in my projects and in th well-being of my team. I have really enjoyed working with Agustín and his method."

QUIQUE DACOSTA,

3-star Michelin chef and entrepreneur

"Today, the FASE method is part of my life. It is a set of habits and systems that have become part of me, and this is what marks the big difference: a method that has enabled me to live a more balanced life, where the time invested is directly proportional to my objectives, both personal and professional."

NEKANE RODRÍGUEZ DE GALARZA,

managing director of Lee Hecht Harrison global affiliates

"As a manager, it's very easy to get side-tracked with multiple tasks and meetings and, as a result, lose focus on what is really important. Applying the FASE method helps you to focus on what delivers a positive impact on your results. And as the whole team implemented the FASE method, it helped everyone to align around the same objectives. It sets off a cascade within the company with everyone working towards achieving common goals."

BEATRIZ VALENTÍ,
Europe managing director of QBE Insurance

"This book is a professional development manual for executives. If you apply it, the results will be immediate results in terms of your effectiveness, freeing up time and the quality of work. The mere act of learning how to focus your attention on the truly important objectives and helping your team to do the same will change the way you have been working until now: what is urgent can wait, but what can't wait is what really matters."

LUIS BARROS,
Digital Business Director – MEDIASET Group

"Agustín has helped us to reach our greatest potential as an architecture firm. By applying his method, we have been able to streamline our processes and the highly varied tasks that we face day-to-day. Amid the frenetic pace, we have built-in sessions for quality time and concentration that are vital for our work."

JAIME SALVÁ,
managing partner of SALVÁ architecture firm

"Agustín himself is a walking example of the effectiveness of this method. Following his way of implementing you will improve efficiency and productivity. In my case, after embedding the four pillars of the method and putting them into action, I have found time for my key priorities, which have been clearly demonstrated in my results. The method has also had a significant impact on my well-being, as well as those around me, including both family and friends, colleagues and collaborators."

AGUSTÍN RODRÍGUEZ,
managing partner of PFS Group

"In the management of SMEs, there is a risk of permanent multitasking, confusing urgent matters with important matters, and the lack of long-term vision. The FASE method is essential, offering a time management method that anchors you in what is really important, triggering an immediate leap in efficiency and productivity, both in work and personal settings."

JOSEP RUBIO,
manager of Rubio Valentines

"Agustín Peralt's FASE method is a highly recommended guide for anyone who wants to improve their productivity as a manager and, at the same time, their quality of life. It is a comprehensive, simple and practical method! Comprehensive because it addresses all the necessary elements to really drive change, simply because it is easy to follow and practical because it is tremendously pragmatic, enabling results from day one."

MARTA VERNET,
marketing director at Idilia Foods

"The FASE method has been the key to my professional growth. It is the antidote to the frustration of being "busy" without getting the results you want within the timeframe you want."

DONATUS GRICIUS,
marketing manager UpSkill Digital

"Despite dedication and years of experience, my multiple responsibilities and work trips were starting to trigger stress and a feeling of being out of control. Thanks to the FASE method, I have gained a feeling of greater proficiency in my work, more control and organization and, consequently, greater enjoyment of my free time."

DR. ANA MELLADO,
dentist, professor and member of the board of directors of SEPES

"In the world of attorneys, we always say that professional development and personal productivity methods can't be implemented in our sector. But the reality is that we are shielding behind the demands and emergencies of our clients to hide our inefficiencies and bad habits. Fortunately, this book, and its author, have managed to prove the opposite. In our particular case, there has been a step-change in the way we work."

VICENTE SANZ-TORRO,
partner ANDERSEN lawyers and law professor
at the University of Valencia

"Agustín offers a culture of working for individuals and teams to lead and manage their time intelligently and efficiently: understanding the dimension and importance of the projects in your in-tray, prioritising them and planning each phase, working to the 20-80 rule, changing bad habits and putting rituals in place that help you to gain more control, reduce stress, concentrate on the important matters and achieve better results. It requires discipline and perseverance but, as Agustín says the rewards will arrive."

CRISTINA OLABARRIA,
marketing director at ESADE Business School a
nd executive committee member.

"In the world of architecture, the creative process and clients' demands are often, a pretext for all kinds of inefficiencies and disorganisation. However, the FASE method is a clear example of how creativity and order coexist. It is a simple method that, right from the start, highlights the professional shortcomings and bad habits that need to change. There really is a complete transformation."

LUCÍA OLANO LAFITA,
architect at the Olano Lafita Studio

"Without a doubt, the method works and is highly effective. It manages to draw out the hidden potential that each of us has inside in a straightforward way. As always, an initial dose of discipline and perseverance is needed, but when the whole team achieves this, a culture of high performance and effectiveness is created. Beyond professional settings, it is also applicable to other areas of life such as social life and sport etc."

FERNANDO QUINTANA,
managing director of the Quimialmel Group

"This book and method not only helped me to improve my organisation, but also my team's system of working. I managed to boost my productivity and make the most of my time, spending it on what really matters and achieving the work-life balance I had always wanted. While it's true that you have to follow the method strictly at the beginning, the feeling of control and mastery is unique. This is the definitive personal productivity method that everyone needs to follow. It is a book to recommend."

ENRIQUE CALABUIG,
CEO of KAIHO and board member of Big Ban Angels

"In the FASE method, women business leaders have found a tool to boost their professional productivity, achieve the desired results and efficiently manage their time. The four pillars represent a method that is easy and simple, helping you, among other things, to focus your attention on what really matters, align the objectives to pursue with your team, limit distractions and plan effectively. Ultimately, all this helps you to strike a better balance between your professional and personal life."

SUSANA SANCHIZ CABANA,
director of Project Promociona ESADE
at the Spanish Confederation of Business Organizations (CEOE)

"This method has been a game-changer in a much-needed and desired transformation, both on a personal level and in the executive team in our company. Its simplicity, adaptability, and above all, ability to deliver results in the short term have been vital. We are like a different team, much more productive, disciplined and focused once we implemented the FASE method. Personally, I have a new sense of mastery over the situation, planning and focus, which helps me to manage my schedule much more effectively and tackle all the challenges in a much more positive and productive way."

VICENTE REMOLÍ,
general manager of Grupotec

"FASE is a practical method that has helped my team and me to increase our individual performance, coordinate better, and reduce stress. We are now a better team."

JUAN PLANES,
board member of Pollos Planes

"My career took a major leap when I decided to move from the public to the private sector: bringing lawsuits, leading and coordinating teams, managing budgets, commercial actions... Agustín's book and his FASE method have shown me how to systematically manage my time, offering solutions to all the problems I have had to face, and I have gained productivity, peace of mind, and self-confidence."

JAVIER GÓMEZ-FERRER,
legal director at BDO Lawyers and Tax Advisors

"After reading the book and learning the FASE method, my transformation began, both in my personal and professional life. Implementing the method properly has enabled me to take charge of this change process. I have gained in efficiency and productivity, I make better decisions, I don't lose focus on what really matters, and I have reduced my stress. Agustín's method is not just the foundation of my transformation as a person; it has also helped me to improve the management of my executive team and the organisation of the company as a whole."

ARANTXA BERNADÍ,
CEO of Bernadí

"With the FASE method, we have managed to maximise the efficiency and effectiveness of the whole team. It is a democratic method that keeps us all on the same page. It is holistic and embraces both the personal and the professional, and has made it easier for us to implement a hybrid working policy. This robust and results-focused method is completely adaptable to changes of setting within the organisation."

CARMEN TOUS,
director of La Font, Agrolimen Group

Going through the FASE program with Juanjo and Agustin had a great value to me, allowing to RETHINK about my reason to be, what to focus on and what not to focus on and delegate to team members that would be best suited to conduct this or that initiative successfully. Even more, it reminded me about the importance of permanently recharging batteries and keeping the right level of own energy in order to increase my efficiency, create a meaningful impact but even more to best inspire and enable my teams to create their own impact."

GUY BOONE,
Corporate Vice President, Global Head of Adhesives
for Consumers & Craftsmen at Henkel

Lead Yourself

Lead Yourself

The FASE® method book

The definitive method to become + productive

Agustín Peralt, Ph.D.

Plataforma Editorial

Original title *Lidérate*
originally published in Spanish in 2015 by Plataforma Editorial

First English edition: May 2023

Plataforma Editorial
c/ Muntaner, 269, entlo. 1ª – 08021 Barcelona
Tel.: (+34) 93 494 79 99
www.plataformaeditorial.com
info@plataformaeditorial.com

Legal deposit: B 7042-2023
ISBN: 978-84-19655-40-0
IBIC: VS

Printed in Spain

Front cover and photocomposition by:
Grafime

The paper used to make this book comes from
controlled forest exploitation where the ecological and social values
are respected, as is the sustainable development of the forest.

Printing:
Podiprint

Contents

FOR MY MOTHER, FOR BEING ROLE MODEL.
For my brother Clemente, for his support.
For my two sons, for their patience
and enthusiasm for this book.

Foreword

By definition, we continually complicate our lives. We convolute what is simple by nature and add complexity to things that can be done more simply. As a general rule, I think we are far from living in an efficient and effective way. This diverts us from our aim of achieving greater results and at the same time greater personal satisfaction.

Over the course of my career, I have met some brilliant professionals, many of them inspiring, and others with high levels of emotional intelligence who were able to get the best from their team. Almost all of them had a high level of integrity and the vast majority were results-focused to achieve the ambitions of the company.

However, not many were able to be proficient right across the board. In order to be able to achieve that, not only would it require a great amount of talent, but also for you to be incredibly efficient and successful in being able to focus on prioritising and using your time appropriately. As Steven Covey rightly pointed out, the main thing is that what really matters really is the main thing.

And this tends to be a scarce quality. Some, very few,

have this instinctively, the rest of us need to work on it. And having a method to do this is a great start.

Today, I continue to be surprised by the fact that effective time management is not a core subject at college level. Much effort is dedicated to teaching knowledge and content but there is very little on how to leverage them effectively.

And the same tends to happen in companies and organizations. All efforts go towards defining improvements in processes (which helps), but rarely is enough invested into strengthening the key competence of self-leadership, which can be a decisive factor in the effectiveness of the organization.

One of the most resounding universal truths, which may seem almost too obvious, is that time is the scarcest resource we have, and what's more, we can't buy it. We are increasingly finding ourselves running out of time.

And there we are, dedicating endless hours to irrelevant issues, unproductive meetings and needless discussions, allowing all sorts of distractions to interfere with our routine.

I met Agustín at a conference in ESADE Business School in Barcelona. I was very impressed by his pragmatism on the issue of time management and the thoroughness with which he had developed his FASE method, touching on all the possible variables in great depth. But Agustín is not just another expert among many. Not only is he incredibly knowledgeable on the subject but his positive energy and attitude are truly contagious. His passion inspires groups and, above all, mobilizes individuals.

Knowing Agustín, I'm sure readers will enjoy this book.

NARCÍS ROURA,
General Manager of PepsiCo, Southern Europe

Introduction

> "In a short space of time, you can emerge from the deepest abyss, the most absolute personal and professional chaos, into a happy and balanced life."

I could sum up the last few years of my life with this phase. In January 2012, at a time of unprecedented levels of unemployment in Spain, I was fired from the company where I had worked for ten years as an executive, and I had to reinvent myself professionally from a place of self-leadership.

It is often said that when you are able to overcome a serious personal and professional crisis, you should count this as a success. This certainly reflects my experience and being able to look at it from a distance now, I can consider that period as a gift that enabled me to transform myself on every level and achieve the life I had always wanted.

In order to work through such a difficult situation, I decided to turn to self-leadership which meant taking responsibility for my part in dealing with the challenging circumstances that I was faced with. Moreover, self-leadership also involves being more effective and efficient to achieve better results, in other words, being more productive. The challenge was a tough one, but not impossible. My first task was to change my mindset and take on the responsibility of becoming my own leader. The second step involved learning from reading all that the experts in the field had published, which meant studying all that was available to me, regarding productivity and time management.I read many authors, all experts on these issues, such as Chris Bailey, Tor Refsland, Leo Babauta and Cal Newport. I analyzed different methods of working such as that of David Allen's *Getting Things Done*, Brian Tracy's *Eat That Frog* and many others that I will discuss throughout this book. I noticed, however, that there was an excess of theoretical discussions and explanations as to why some things may or may not work in many of the books or, at times, an overload of technical and over-complicated language that could not be interpreted easily. Other books, whilst presenting excellent theories, lacked in their exploration of practical and effective exercises that I could apply in the real world in order to manage my time more effectively. So much had been written about the right mindset to drive transformation and improvement, as well as the steps needed to achieve it, but there was no concrete and simple methodology that I could apply, day-to-day, to improve this key skill of self-leadership. I needed what one of my clients, a company director, termed brilliantly: "A simple, straightforward, action-oriented method". I needed a system that would boost productivity and yield results fast. A guide that would set out the main objectives or issues to resolve, including regular procedures to review your progress and stay on track. And because nothing like this had been done before, I decided to create it.

> "Keep going until something stops you, then keep going. Hold firmly to your aspirations; tenacity breeds tenacity as success breeds success."
> **DEBRA A. BENTON**

And this is how the FASE method came into being. All the theoretical knowledge I was gradually gaining as well as the practical experience I had acquired over the years inspired me to develop my own method and system of working. The result was the creation of a comprehensive method that offers a range of tools to set important objectives that you can then transfer to a daily plan. You will consequently be able to achieve your objectives in a gradual and sustainable way, striking the right balance between your personal and professional life.

The name of this method, FASE, is based on the four pillars or phases involved: **focus, attention, systemization** and **energy**- the four basic building blocks:

- **Focus** on what is really matters to achieve your goals. This means managing your time well and letting go of habits that lead to a distracted or aimless way of working without a clear direction.

- **Attention or full absorption in order** to make the most of your time and carry out each task efficiently with no distractions. Deep concentration and focus at certain points throughout the day is needed to tackle complex and relevant tasks.
- **Systematization** daily, weekly and monthly rituals and habits to embed the method into your life in a natural and sustainable way. This is not just about professional habits, it is also important to schedule key elements such as rest, meal times and exercise to improve our performance.
- **Energy** to achieve our optimum state throughout the day. Once you establish the right routines, you will have more energy to leverage, helping to make your daily challenges more achievable.

I developed the FASE method, drawing on the following elements:

- Studying and observing renowned experts in the field of productivity such as Brian Tracy, Steven Covey and David Allen. As a visiting professor at HVA University in Amsterdam, I also had the opportunity to observe the working practices in Holland. In my view, the Dutch are masters of productivity and effectiveness, and we have much to learn from them.
- My experience of working as an executive and the profound

crisis I experienced over a three-year period during which my professional problems were compounded by some personal struggles.
- The relationship with clients who have implemented my method, including executives, lawyers, entrepreneurs and architects, all of whom have been a source of immense knowledge.
- My consultancy work with companies in 2020 to facilitate remote working during the Coronavirus pandemic.

Over time, having seen that the method I had created for my own self-development, would also be valid and of use to the individuals and companies, I worked with., encouraged me to write the book so that anyone, anywhere, could apply the method without my input. I also intend to include, in this updated version, a new section on remote working which, for many people, is a new reality that is, without a doubt, here to stay. Therefore, the book you are now reading is the result of the method that I developed to kickstart my productivity and it will be useful for you however you work, whether 100 % office-based, 100 % remotely or a combination of both.

This book is the book for you if you are dealing with any of the following issues:

- You are experiencing serious difficulties in your working life.
- You are dealing with stressful situations in your personal life.

- You urgently need to increase your productivity at work.
- You manage a team and you want to learn more about effectiveness and productivity techniques to lead by example.
- You find it hard to be effective while working remotely.
- You want to develop self-leadership as a key professional skill.

Are constantly over complicatingmain goalwere hadandamazedit can't be boughtmanagers The FASE method is a tool that teaches you:

- how to work efficiently and effectively, eliminate distractions and bad habits, and focus on what really matters to achieve the goals that you have set for yourself.
- how to manage your energy proactively, an essential component to improving productivity, while systematizing a series of routines to avoid constant overexertion.
- how to develop big ideas or visualize where you want to be in two or three years. I will teach you how to set a series of objectives and draft action plans that will help you will achieve the personal and professional life you desire.

The FASE method is easy to understand and implement, helping you to achieve extraordinary results in a short space of time through daily and weekly plans and actions. You will also gain back more free time to spend with family and friends or pursue hobbies. Furthermore, as well as eliminating the stress caused by chaos, disorganization and anxiety, you will be able to feel balanced and happier as a result, both personally and professionally.

Improving our lives depends on us, and this is something we need to keep top of mind. Keep reading and you will discover a method that many people are already using to achieve more, reduce stress and feel more in control.

> "I don't divide the world into the weak and the strong,
> or the successes and the failures, those who make it or those who don't.
> I divide the world into learners and non-learners."
> **BENJAMIN BARBER**

1. The key to making changes successfully

A mindset for change

> "When you're overwhelmed, take a moment and write a list of the pending issues that concern you. List the things we calm, helps us get worries out of our heads and guide us on what we should focus on."
>
> **PAULA RIZZO**

Many of us work intensely and enthusiastically, but few manage to keep stress at bay or the anxious feeling of not having enough hours in the day to get everything done. In my case, it wasn't until I found myself submerged in a major crisis, that I realized I was unhappy and overwhelmed at work and how this was negatively impacting my personal life. A few friends had even already told me, in no uncertain terms, that this was no way to live but I was feeling paralyzed. It was as if I was experiencing Stockholm syndrome, convinced that there was no solution beyond continuing to work obsessively.

As I mentioned before, when I finally hit rock bottom, I decided to spend a long time learning about the resources that would help me to set goàls, define strategies and find a way of working to achieve a healthier personal and professional future, as well as attaining the productivity I desired. In the end, what started as a mere way of trying to survive became my passion and eventually my profession.

The mixture of all of the theoretical and practical knowledge that I acquired along the way helped me to truly transform my life. My career, which until then had been in senior management, took a complete turnabout. I became a university professor, started mentoring senior managers and developed the FASE method. A method that has helped many people to improve their time management, boost productivity, and above all achieve the personal and professional happiness that they all want and deserve.

When I realized that I had to get my life in order to tackle the complex situation that I was mired in, I understood that planning would be key. We all know that managing our time well, leads to better professional outcomes and better quality of life. However, we are all too often, exposed to an overload of information in today's society and more and more of us are online 24-7. This, in turn, demands an extra amount of effort and time management on our part, due to the distractions and bad habits developed by our addictions to technology. Nevertheless, we are more capable of overcoming these obstacles and taking on major challenges than we think. I am not just saying this, just to motivate you, dear reader, it is a reality that I have seen demonstrated in recent years. The problem is that we often don't tackle these obstacles and challenges with the right mindset, which would ensure both a good start and a sense of sustained discipline over time, driving us towards success.

So, the key is to follow a methodology that provides a strategic work plan, enabling you to systematize and organize your time optimally. To do this, it is essential that you answer the following three questions before you start the process:

- What is your key objective?
- What method are you going to follow to ensure that you stay on track in your everyday life?
- Are you willing to be disciplined to make this method part of your life so that it becomes like second nature?

Once you have answered these three questions, you'll be ready to start the process of change with every chance of success.

Stop making excuses and achieve your dreams

"Agustín, you are a real pro… at finding excuses for everything." This is exactly what a good friend said to me when I was trying to convince him that I had no time to read books. This is probably one of the most impactful comments

I have heard in my professional life and, since then, I've always taken into account my share of the responsibility in resolving any given problem. So, think twice when you find yourself complaining about not having enough time to do something…

It's very difficult to come across an executive or professional who says they have enough time to do what they want to do. The few I have met were people with two key traits: they had clearly identified their 80/20 – the 20 % of tasks that contribute to 80 % of the results.

They are also disciplined because they know that their results depend exclusively on their own proactivity, planning and effort. In other words, they have stopped making excuses and trying to blame external circumstances. Their ability to plan, systematize and ritualize daily and weekly habits have enabled them to reach their main goals. This is what differentiates these people from others; and you can easily see that they don't have any amazing superpowers, except for their ability to plan and their hard work.

On the other hand, there are those that you could say are the Kings of the excuse-makers; those who believe their own lies and have convinced themselves that they "can't keep up" but who have spent years with bad working habits and no productive routines. These people live stressed-out lives and end up regretting not having achieved what they had set out to, and ultimately, living with their unfulfilled dreams. The problem is that fear of the unknown can paralyze us, leaving us struggling to escape the cycle of frenetic action, with no system and poor results. You may be working long hours but with nothing to show for it. For many years, I was one of these people and the worst part is that this situation is detrimental not only for you but also for the people in your personal life.

There are also people who don't suffer from stress but who feel deeply unsatisfied in life because they are not happy in their professional lives. They were able to identify what they should do to make the necessary changes, but they complain about not having enough time to do anything about it. In these cases, their problems are not caused by having an all-too-consuming job but because they allowed their time to be taken up by non-productive activities such as going on social media, watching TV or they lack the willpower to take the necessary steps that lead to a life of fulfilment. And so, weeks, months, years and even a whole lifetime go by, without ever having reached their full potential or some kind of happiness.

If you find yourself stuck in such a position, like being trapped in a maze, with no way out, take a step back to observe and analyse the situation.

A road map towards change: the mind map technique

When I started the process of getting my life in order and reinventing myself professionally, I was battling on so many fronts that the first thing I needed to do was to take stock of my situation and create a road map towards change. To do this, I used the mind map technique, with a pen and paper, because what can seem like an insurmountable problem in our minds can transform into something much more manageable on paper.

Tony Buzan's[1] mind map technique is a very useful tool to use to reflect and generate ideas. It also helps you to understand and resolve problems, acts as a guide to outline a series of plans and actions, helps improve concentration, and enables you to measure your progress.

Mind maps are a framework with the main idea placed at the centre and you keep adding secondary ideas or other relevant themes around this, using different colours for each idea.

My first mind map reflected a general overview of the issues I had to resolve (work and finances), without ever losing sight of the various aspects of my personal life.

Big problems are broken down into small actions

When you break down a goal into smaller actions, or a problem into different areas, and then look at it as a whole, it is much easier to analyze and plan the tasks that you will need to carry out to achieve your goal.

In my case, both breaking the problem down and setting aside a bit of time every day to work on it helped to keep

1. Tony Buzan, *The Mind Map Book: Unlock Your Creativity, Boost Your Memory, Change Your Life* (BBC Active 2009)

me motivated and took the pressure off. Even better, I was able to work in a balanced way and I progressed in each one of my goals without neglecting any of them.

The act of setting small, daily goals also helps you to focus more on what you have achieved as opposed to what you still need to do, which adds extra motivation to the activity. In addition, dedicating some time every day (even a little) to each one of these issues can lead to significant progress over time. You should never underestimate how much you can progress on daily basis, even if it seems insignificant.

These mind maps-or action plans- are useless, unless there is a system behind them that involves dedicating enough time and consistency to your objectives. That is to say, you need to have a system of weekly and daily planning in line with your mind map and objectives.

For this to work, it's essential to have a method that drives you to be proactive and leads to maximum productivity. All this contributes to a greater awareness of what needs to be done in each area of your life, better results and effectiveness, and in turn, brings personal and professional satisfaction.

I had so many issues to tackle that trying to solve them without a large dose of productivity and strategic planning would have meant certain failure. My mind map helped me to see that I would be able to reinvent myself professionally and highlighted the need to be productive and organized to get everything done. This was what led me to develop a daily and weekly system of working, a method that would help me to become efficient, make the best use of time and concentrate on the most important issues. So, every week I would set myself some tasks for the following week and I was able to keep track of the progress I had made during the previous week. As well as doing this, I made a point of recording everything in a table where I updated my progress and that really motivated me to keep going.

How to make a mind map of your life

The central idea needs to have a title – I called mine "My new life" – and around this idea, you will need to add the categories or aspects relevant to your life, however obvious they may seem. Then, for each one of these categories, note down a number of objectives that will guide the weekly planning of your next activities. For example, my categories were:

- Children
- Work
- Family
- Friends
- Finances

There are many more possible categories to use such as a spouse, in-laws, hobbies, savings, assets, personal growth, and so on.

The next step is to set your goals for the next trimester or semester for each one of these categories. For example:

"help my children with their homework so that they can improve in the subjects that they are struggling with" or "plan weekend activities with them". Alternatively, you can also create a mind map of the key issues at this stage of your life or your main priorities.

A quick snapshot of my mind map and the associated goals was:

- Children: win joint custody.
- Assets: address my difficult financial circumstances.
- Work: reinvent myself.
- Me: achieve high levels of physical, emotional and cognitive energy.

You should remember that achieving major objectives requires a great deal of planning and a series of small actions which, over time, will make up the whole project. In much the same way that building a bridge involves a whole series of detailed action plans and dedication that give shape to this great feat of civil engineering, rebuilding our personal and professional lives - particularly when we are starting from zero, or in my case, minus one – involves consistently setting small daily, weekly, monthly, and quarterly objectives. The key to success is in the methodology that we use to ensure that we are meeting the targets we have set ourselves every day. These objectives haven't been imposed by a manager or superior, you only have yourself to answer to, so consistency and dedication are essential. Once you have a mind map committed to paper and a good diary where you note down your mini objectives, almost without realizing it, you will begin to achieve results that only a few months earlier you wouldn't have thought possible. However, when it comes to planning and checking our daily, weekly and monthly activities an Excel spreadsheet is better.

On the next page, you will find a template of the cells and columns I used in my FASE diary that we will explore in detail in the section on focus. HIT refers to the high impact tasks linked to this objective.

Do you know what your element is?

As I explained earlier, one of the main goals in my mind map was to reinvent myself professionally and find a new job. To do this, I made use of an exercise in the book *Finding Your Element* by Ken Robinson.[2] His approach is extremely useful in helping us to discover what we want to pursue in life as a career.

I strongly recommend reading this book in times of crisis or transformation in your professional life. Its reflections offer a coherent framework to help us to find our mission in life and stop our emotional state of mind from tripping us up.

2. Finding Your Element: How to Discover Your Talents and Passions and Transform Your Life, (Penguin, 30 Jan.2014)

Objectives and HIT **Month**

	OBJECTIVES	HIT 1	HIT 2	HIT 3...
1	Improve my Business English	Contratar un profesor 1-1 Business English in English	Read Harvard articles 20mns/day	Watch series
2				
3				
4				
5				
6				
7				
8				

Objectives and HIT **Month**

	OBJECTIVES	HIT 1	HIT 2	HIT 3...
1				
2				
3				
4				
5				
6				
7				
8				

This exercise is centered on the importance of reflecting on what really drives us professionally, taking our various skills and unique aptitudes into account.

The element is defined as "the meeting point between natural aptitudes that make you stand out and personal passions and drives".

Finding your element involves delving deep into your inner world through a series of questions and turning to others who know you well so that you can really discover yourself. We often don't stop to think about what really matters to us; instead, it's as if we are on autopilot, letting it determine the course of our professional life. Robinson also reflects on the qualities that the labor market values the most among the scores of job seekers. As such, your element must be the combination of what you feel passionate about and your particular aptitudes and abilities, as well as being in line with the demands of the current labor market.

After my crisis, my first thoughts revolved around the idea of not returning to the business world as an executive; instead I wanted to focus on teaching, training and helping improve the skills of other professionals. I liked the idea of helping others by contributing everything I had learned in while working in the business world and teaching was something that I'd always been interested in. In the past, when I had given lectures and workshops in universities and business schools, I had always received positive feedback on my ability to connect and communicate with people. All this led me to consider that I had certain unique abilities when it came to communicating with others, motivating them and supporting them to grow professionally. Another advantage I could add to this new career direction, was the fact that, being fluent in English, I was also able to teach in the language and this put me in a unique position when it came to labor market demands. In Spain, finding a lecturer with experience of working as a director as well as being able to teach in English is not an easy task.

As you read this, you may think it was all very simple but the reality is that it came as the result of a much more complex process of reflection. But I had confidence in what I was doing and during the tough times, self-assurance is vital. When it seemed as though all doors had slammed shut, a window gradually opened, offering me inspiration and hope. I had a very clear vision of the goal I wanted to achieve.

Get ready for the challenge ahead (or fake it until you make it)

Sometimes, even though we have a clear idea and believe in ourselves, we can fall prey to what Daniel Goleman calls "emotional hijacking" in his acclaimed books on emotional intelligence.[3]

3. Daniel Goleman, *Emotional Intelligence: Why it Can Matter More Than IQ* (New York: Bantam Books, 1995)

When we fall victim to emotional hijacking, our limbic system disables all the brain's mechanisms to carry out functions that, under normal circumstances, we would be perfectly capable of managing. This hijacking causes an immediate reaction in the pre-frontal cortex – the part of the brain associated with rational thinking – causing us to lose perspective and struggle to think clearly, which in turn generates more fear and prevents us from tackling even the most uncomplicated of situations. In situations where we are fighting against ourselves, the last thing we should do is give up, as this will only delay the moment of truth. So, remind yourself that you are more than capable, be brave and get ready for the challenge.

So, there you have it, nothing beats the potential of good preparation. In my case, when I started teaching, the basic idea of having to face a class of fifteen students triggered all of my fears. My fragile emotional state of mind left me temporarily paralyzed, so I decided to tackle every university class with obsessive preparation. And, along with my efforts and dedication, the number of classes I taught increased to the extent that, nine months later I was offered a part time teaching contract.

During this period, I learned to mask my inner state of mind, as the psychologist Amy Cuddy[4] discusses in her book. If the university had known how I was really feeling, it is

4. Amy Cuddy, *Presence: Bringing Your Boldest Self to Your Biggest Challenges* (Orion, 2016)

unlikely they would have given me any kind of opportunity.[5] I also learned that putting in extra effort to prepare will help you to overcome any temporary incapacities. I planned my classes meticulously, but my physical and emotional states were working against me. There were many moments when I thought about throwing the towel in, but enthusiasm, hope and patience helped me to keep going. There were good times and bad. For example, some of the students that I came across tried to take advantage when they saw that I was in a fragile state, while others, with whom I was honest about my problems, met my vulnerability with great understanding and humanity. Gradually, the situation began to improve, and I discovered that there is nothing more motivating than doing a job you love. The initial reflection on my element had been key, and that is why, when I taught and started to feel good, my motivation soared: the combination of my sense of duty and dedication were almost perfect. Every day, I would demand a little more of myself and, because I was doing something I felt passionate about, this gave me the motivation to chase the next opportunity.

These days, I like to define what I discovered during that period in the following way: "From a very young age, I always enjoyed helping people to become happier. But I had to go through a serious personal and professional crisis in order to discover my passion and to be able to make a living

5. On this point, Amy Cuddy believes that masking anxiety, and even appearing self-more aware as well as persevering, helps to achieve objectives

from it. Now, I am able to coach and advise others who want to add value to their professional lives, either as students, employees or entrepreneurs. I no longer say that 'I have to work'; I am actually enjoying myself and being paid for the privilege. Nothing is more rewarding for me now than the work I do day to day. For me, every day feels like Friday."

Describe your vision of the future (don't forget your personal life)

The next step of my journey back then was to describe my vision of the future two or three years from then, based on my understanding of the definition of my element. The description of the vision was important because it helped me to flesh out the ideas that would guide me, as I mapped out concrete and coherent action plans that could be implemented immediately and that would drive me towards achieving my goals.

So, to get started, you need to create a clear image in your mind of the goal you want to achieve, for example: In what way do you wish to transform your professional (or personal) life? Or, which major issues or challenges do you need to tackle? Write everything down so that you have greater control over your project and make a commitment to yourself.

To turn your vision into reality, the three key elements are: identifying your objective, sketching out the plans in your mind map and having an iron-clad discipline every day. Brendon Burchard's excellent book *The Charge,*[6] sums it up in three words: desire, direction and discipline.

On a professional level, this approach is not only useful but also reassuring because it organizes your mind and encourages a positive outlook. That said, any process in which our emotions dominate the stage is always trickier to navigate. Nonetheless, when you face a classes meticulously, but my physical and emotional states were working against me. There were many moments when I thought about throwing the towel in, but enthusiasm, hope and patience helped me to keep going. There were good times and bad. For example, some of the students that I came across tried to take advantage when they saw that I was in a fragile state, while others, with whom I was honest about my problems, met my vulnerability with great understanding and humanity. Gradually, the situation began to improve, and I discovered that there is nothing more motivating than doing a job you love. The initial reflection on my element had been key, and that is why, when I taught and started to feel good, my motivation soared: the combination of my sense of duty and dedication was almost perfect. Every day, I would demand a little more of myself and, because I was doing something I felt new professional challenge or you need to deal with a problem at work it is always a good idea to start from a reflection taking your personal objectives into

6. The Charge: Activating the 10 Human Drives That Make You Feel Alive

account, otherwise your personal life might suffer as a result, if you end up neglecting it. Having a balanced personal life is crucial as it will also empower you to tackle professional challenges with greater strength. Remember: *mens sana in corpore sano (Healthy mind in a healthy body).* So, make sure your mind map also includes a section on how to improve your personal life.

My personal life was my Achilles heel. I wanted to feel happy in my new family set up: divorced with two children whom I adore and who deserved the best version of me. Once again, my best allies were two of the simplest but the most powerful and effective tools: pen and paper. Writing is much more powerful than you may realize. It clarifies our ideas, eliminates anxiety about the future and motivates us to complete projects (yes, I never tire of repeating this because, despite how simple it may be, we don't seem to write things down enough, because we may be terrified of staring at a blank page).

> "Each semester, write down what you would like to achieve in the next six months. In addition, it identifies the barriers or problems you may encounter and write about. What are you going to do to cope with them?"
>
> **DANIEL PINK**

To resolve my problematic situation, I needed to get practical and go straight to the point. My mission was to become a coach and mentor for executives and university and post-graduate students while maintaining a level of income similar to what I was earning as an executive. But, now, I also wanted to be happy and go to work with a spring in my step, while enjoying spending quality time with my family and friends. So, I got into the habit of creating a quarterly mind map that, as well as my professional goals, also included areas of my personal life, such as activities and projects with my children or future plans with my partner. This idea continues to help me each week as I reflect on all the important areas of my life from a place of calm and come up with a series of actions that are consistent with my personal and professional goals. For example, I am continuing to improve my fitness levels, which, in turn, improves my professional performance and boosts my energy levels required to make the desired changes.

Frequency is key

Nothing is more useful than dedicating some time every day to work on the goal you have set yourself, in order to progress and improve in any area. If you are consistent, even by just spending thirty minutes a day on your goal, the results can be truly spectacular, and you will see that there is always enough time to tackle anything you set your mind to.

In most processes of trying to overcome major obstacles, the planning stage is usually logical and easy to put down on paper, however, when it comes to putting the plan into action, things can get complicated. In most cases, what often sets successful people apart from others is their ability to take action and to keep it up day after day, week after week. And if we want to really hone our effectiveness, it is crucial to have a concrete methodology to help us be productive time and again.

In my case, the objective I set myself was to obtain my doctorate. Every day, I spent at least thirty minutes, and sometimes up to three hours, on this and, as a result, this was my the greatest challenge and cognitive effort. I achieved a doctorate in business and management in only three and a half years and I'm sure that there are others more knowledgeable than me that had to spend ten years doing this, instead. Consistency and discipline can yield a level of performance that we would never have thought possible.

Going the extra mile effort at the last minute

Robin Sharma, one of the most renowned professional growth experts, talks about the "extra mile effort" concept in his fantastic book *The Leader Who Had No Title*:[7] that final effort that makes all the difference.

Personally, what often helped me to make that final push was the fear of failure or of missing out on a good opportunity.

7. Robin Sharma, *The Leader Who Had No Title: A Modern Fable on Real Success in Business and in Life* (Simon & Schuster, 2010)

The pressure of having to perform successfully usually generates this extra mile effort that will most likely result in success. For example: A final check over my notes before I began a class, that extra effort with a client who wasn't making progress and following up with them outside 'office hours', or helping a student with a career challenge, all of which brought some kind of reward. The rewards that this extra effort bring are crucial in encouraging positive thinking and motivating us to do better in the future and developing willpower.

The key elements in creating change

After two and a half years of effort and perseverance, it was clear that my personal and professional reinvention was becoming a reality. My relationship with my children and my connection with my friends were all that I had hoped for. Professionally, I was now able to do a job I was actually enjoying, I had financial stability and was able to maintain the Life standard I had aimed for. So, in the summer of 2014, on a quiet hike up the local mountains, I started to reflect on the key elements that had helped me overcome my crisis. The following main points are the conclusions I was able to reach:

Confidence

I had always been able to put faith in myself- even if I didn't always feel it, at times- and in my ability to overcome any difficulties. In spite of the economic crisis that had hit the country, at the time, I trusted that I would be able to find a new career path, specifically, in education. I was able to keep an optimistic, yet realistic outlook on life, which enabled me to work hard and with discipline.

Honesty and Receptiveness

I learned to open up and to accept the support of those around me by being honest about my situation and my feelings. What's more important, I wasn't afraid to expose my vulnerability, which meant that I was open to receiving advice from many sources. This proved to be crucial in helping me make the necessary changes to evolve as a person.

Discipline

I invested a lot of time, in a systematic way, into staying physically and emotionally strong. Had I not done so, I wouldn't have been able to deal with the challenges and I would have probably ended up drained.

Efficiency

I consciously decided to become highly productive and efficient. This, in turn, helped me to consistently achieve small wins that encouraged me to keep fighting.

Validity

Right from the beginning, I believed in the productivity method that I had developed, the FASE method, was going to be beneficial for many professionals, because it had already helped me. There was something in my personal and professional experience that would be valuable for other people, and this was fundamental in driving my professional reinvention.

The results spoke for themselves:

I went from a vicious circle to a virtuous circle. In 2014 I was voted the best postgraduate professor among over 400 teachers, in 2015 I obtained my doctorate and by the end of the same year, I had built up a portfolio of clients and projects which left no room for doubt, my consulting and executive mentoring business was solid.

> "Your level of success is determined by your level of discipline and perseverance."
>
> **ANONYMOUS**

As is often the case in life, professional challenges gain their true meaning when we show our most human and authentic side. One such case is a call I received from the husband of one of my clients that I will never forget. He called to tell me that I'd managed to help his wife and her family to find happiness again after I supported them to improve the running of the family business. There is nothing more satisfying than when a client tells you that they have regained their enthusiasm for their job after many, many years or when an executive tells you that they have managed to reboot their career. All this was and still is, a reaffirmation of the vision of just how much I could offer others.

After all the hard work and perseverance, while struggling against feelings of despondency, my efforts finally paid off. When I analyze my process of transformation, it is clear that working in an ordered and systematic way, following the plan I had designed day by day, week by week and month by month, was the fundamental driver of my success. My self-discipline and ability to take a step back and reflect on a weekly basis, as well as making any necessary changes and acting upon them, were the key elements to my methodology: The FASE method.

2. The key to being 100 % productive

"Time is what we want most, but what we use worst."
WILLIAM PENN

The need to be efficient and effective

During my period of reflection on how I was going to find a solution to all my problems, I remembered the concept that the business and management expert Peter Drucker called "personal productivity".

For Drucker, personal productivity is about achieving efficiency and effectiveness. *Efficiency* is doing things correctly without wasting time, in other words, making the most out of each minute, free from distractions, and working with full concentration. *Effectiveness* is focusing on what really matters to achieve the intended results. It is about doing the right things, the most relevant tasks in a given situation. Therefore, productive people are able to work without distractions, focus their full attention, and assign this quality time to the tasks that are really crucial in terms of achieving the desired outcome. It means doing the right thing in the right way. And when we are *efficient* and *effective*, we become productive which, for Drucker, is what it means to be truly effectual.

In dealing with my own situation, I had to be more productive than ever, as I tackled an array of very complex issues within a short space of time. I needed to reach a high level of both effectiveness and efficiency. Back then, it never really crossed my mind that the model I was creating to achieve this would, in the future, become a tool to coach and build the capacity of other professionals. Sometimes life brings wonderful surprises.

Improve your productivity and be happier

When we get organized, we are more productive because we achieve our objectives while investing less time. This leads not only to an improvement in our professional results but also boosts happiness in our personal life. Bear in mind that happiness is influenced much more by what we do than what we have, especially if what we are doing is meaningful and enables us to make progress. This is why I would encourage you to improve your productivity, even if you are not having problems at work and just want to get the most out of working remotely, or even if there is no obvious compelling reason to do it. Do it for the simple reason that it will most definitely bring happiness because:

- When you develop professionally and achieve better results, you feel more satisfied with your purpose in life, and therefore happier as a result.
- When you manage your time better, you have more spare time for personal.
- When you manage your time better, you have more spare time for personal activities that will, in turn, bring you little boosts of happiness.
- Your level of psychological stress will go down, so will your levels of cortisol which are responsible for generating irritability and sadness.
- Every day you will see how your way of organizing yourself is different to everyone else's. This will bolster you and give you a sense of security.
- You will be able to make the most of remote working or a combination of both and see results.

In order to improve my productivity and bring a sense of focus to the new professional and personal life I was cultivating, I wrote a detailed plan of everything I had to do. Without this, I could easily have lost focus or failed to take the necessary steps at the right time and in the right way. Therefore, drafting a plan of mini objectives that would gradually lead me towards my end goal for each one of the challenges detailed in my mind map was a key task. But a plan involves focusing on each one of the actions, monitoring them, and steadily carrying them out, establishing a working routine. However, as well as a useful methodology that helped to boost my productivity, I realized that I also needed to cultivate a series of important behavioural patterns.

The four Hs that boost your productivity

Whether you start to feel overwhelmed, or want to take a professional leap, or you simply want to claw back some time to spend on other projects or activities, you will become aware of the fact that you need to be more productive. This involves transforming the way you work, making profound changes, to a greater or lesser extent, depending on each given situation.

But whatever your situation, to successfully embed a process of transformation and boost your productivity, there are four 'essential Hs':

Hunger

You need to be determined– hungry for it- that something that drives you, right from the beginning, to start this process of change. This motivation is necessary both to kickstart start the process and to overcome any difficulties you may encounter along the way. The final goal may be anything from getting a promotion, starting a new job or being able to spend more quality time with the family. In each case, there must be something that motivates you to want to make the required effort to change the way you work. This is the WHY and the WHAT FOR that underpins a process such as this.

Honesty

Don't be tempted to self-sabotage and try to convince yourself that the problem lies in your external circumstances, because in all likelihood, the source of the problem resides in your current way of organizing yourself. The psychologist Julian B. Rotter[8] defines the concept of the "internal locus of control (ILC)"[9] versus the "external locus of control (ELC)"[10] as a central personality trait. In a work setting, these two concepts refer to the sense of being in control of your own professional destiny (ILC), versus the belief that external factors determine your development and opportunities for success (ELC). Research shows that people with an ILC are healthier and feel less depressed than those with an ELC.

Remember, it is essential for us all to be honest, starting with ourselves. It is easy to fall into the trap of blaming our low productivity on external factors such as your boss, your sector, your role or even your mobile phone. Similarly, don't be too nice to yourself when you consider the progress you have achieved or whether you are being consistent in your approach to achieving them.

8. Julian B. Rotter, "Internal Versus External control of reinforcement: A case history of a variable", American Psychologist, vol. 45, no.4 (1990): 489

9. Perception that oneself controls one's destiny.

10. Perception that external forces beyond one's personal control determine an individual's destiny.

"Be able to assume the personal responsibility that corresponds to you when things don't work out. In this way, that assumption of responsibility will direct your attention to future actions that you can perform to achieve better results."
PETER BREGMAN

Humility

It is essential for you to be able to stay humble, in the sense that you need to acknowledge that the organizational system you are using, is not working. You must also accept the fact that the right methodology may be completely different or even opposed to your normal way of working. Trust and go with it. Remember that your system hasn't worked so far and you need to try a different one.

Hands-on

You need to have a hands-on attitude, meaning that you need to have an action-focused mindset and be proactive. Without acting daily to tweak and improve your plans, they will be nothing more than good intentions. It's about action, not words. Good ideas without action will only bring disappointment. These actions will also help you to integrate new habits that will become the foundation of your new way of working, and habits need the repetition of routines. When you manage to integrate these habits into your routines, everything in your day-to-day life will be much simpler.

Full concentration: it's not too little time, it's too many distractions

Today, more than ever, time is our most precious resource. Proof of this is the same old excuse- "there is not enough hours in the day". Whether you need to study for an exam, draft a report, or take a vacation, managing your time properly is fundamental. And given that it is becoming increasingly rare, effective time management itself, is fast becoming a skill that sets people apart in the professional world.

A few years ago, it would have been probably difficult to imagine that with the arrival of new technologies such as the internet and smart phones (that in theory were going to boost our capacity) we would be entering into an era with lowest productivity and highest distraction rates in history. The new forms of communication and instant messaging such as email, WhatsApp, Slack, Telegram and iMessage can be particularly detrimental. As I see every day in the companies that I work with, instead of helping us to become more productive and improve our communication, they have become the primary and most damaging time-robbers that have ever existed. On the other hand, nobody could have imagined that this technology would help us to work remotely, with the many advantages that come with a combination of office-based and home-based working. But a technology overload has created what some are referring to as "Zoom fatigue", something that is clearly having a negative impact on our energy.

We are addicted to distractions and are glued to our mobile phones from the minute we wake up in the morning until we go to sleep at night, which has the added effect of delaying the onset of sleep. This constant exposure to distractions and multitasking causes us to waste a lot of time between moving from one task to the next, leaving us unable to concentrate on something for more than ten minutes straight.

"The technology we use has become an obsession, even in a full-blown addiction."
NIR EYAL

Most people acknowledge this situation, but very few are determined to find a solution. Many authors have emphasized this, such as Andy Stalman, in his book *HumanOffOn,*[11] who reminds us that the information overload that we are currently exposed to is nothing in comparison to what awaits us in the future. Robin Sharma also believes that we need moments of "zero connectivity" otherwise it is impossible to concentrate on important tasks that require cognitive abilities.

Over the last two years I have been able to observe executives and business owners in their day to day working lives and, frankly, I have yet to meet a professional who has not been affected by one of the two following problems:

11. Andy Stalman, *HumanOnOff,* (Deusto, 2018).

Wasting time absent-mindedly

We work reactively, drifting aimlessly through the day to day, responding to what other people send us, to the endless possibilities of entertainment from our smartphones, the continuous stream of emails and invitations to join video calls, instead of working proactively on what really matters. If you stopped to think about the amount of time you spend answering emails and WhatsApp messages, checking social media, browsing online reading articles of personal interest and making phone calls, you would be shocked. This is why I make a point of analyzing how my clients use their time during the first stage of the FASE method, in the self-assessment.

The failure to focus on what really matters

There are many professionals that work almost on auto-pilot and are unable to concentrate on the goals that really matter- the ones that bring results. In other words, they are incapable of dedicating time to the real tasks that are actually relevant, at any given moment. Those who manage to escape this behaviour set themselves apart not because of the way they work, but because this way of working leads to results that are almost impossible for others to achieve. They manage to concentrate and focus their full attention on what is truly important are able to progress and achieve results much quicker than people who may have more cognitive capacities and experience than them. This is what I like to master: working with coherent intentionality, frequency and consistency.

Common traits of those who are truly productive people

Truly productive people often share a series of attitudes, behaviors, and values:

- They invest time in observing how they manage their time. They assess themselves, looking at how they have worked, whether they have made the most of the day and they give themselves an appraisal at the end of the day. Similarly, they reflect and plan ahead on a weekly basis.
- They have their own methods of organizing their time and their work and they stick to it consistently, on a daily basis. This enables them to set goals.
- They always have their next goals and challenges in mind, and this motivates them to focus and make the effort to be really productive.
- They have systematized a series of rituals and habits that they review regularly and always keep to, except in extraordinary circumstances.
- They are able to dedicate part of their time to what is really important and decisive to achieve results, and they avoid procrastinating on more complex tasks.
- They have learned to adapt their time management and

method to any working environment, whether in the office, working remotely or a combination of the two. Even when they travel, they dedicate time to improving this without having to improvise or not being able to complete tasks.

Discover what kind of worker you are and get ready for change!

As a result of my experience and observation, I have been able to classify people according to how they work. Identifying yourself with one of these descriptions will help you to zero in on the behaviours you need to change:

- **Brilliant but chaotic:** they are intelligent people, but they do the bare minimum. They tend to achieve results even though they don't have a clear working system. Their personality is somewhat anarchic, they achieve minimum results to avoid getting into trouble and they are not prepared to change the way they work because they feel comfortable. The problem is that they have a great deal of potential but don't manage to get the best out of themselves, in other words, they don't reach peak performance. This is a burden both for the individual and the organization they work for.

- **Dedicated but unfocused:** they are hardworking, but they don't have a focus which means that, despite the many hours that they invest into their work, they don't achieve the desired results. They are the first to arrive in the office and the last to leave. Sometimes their performance stands out, but this is more than often, not the case. And they almost always seem swamped. The problem is that in the long term this system of intense, long hours at the cost of their personal life leads to burnout, and even serious emotional problems because continuous stress comes at a high price.

- **The self-serving shirker:** they do very little work, but they almost always deliver the minimum results to save their own skin. They do whatever they please but when they sense the risk of being exposed, they use their ingenuity to extricate themselves or scrape through on bare minimum results. The problem is that these people tend to sink the morale of their colleagues, who often end up hating them. Eventually, they come into conflict with their managers, who tire of them and their "last-minute solutions" and "saved by the bell" attitude.

- **Productive and astute:** they represent a minority percentage of workers in organizations. They are textbook productive; they have clearly identified their 80/20 – that 20 % of key tasks that yield 80 % of the results – and they are fully focused on this. They work with full attention, know how to say no and eliminate distractions. They always make a detailed plan of their days and weeks. They are proactive and if they think a meeting is not going anywhere, they will say so. They prioritize their physical and emotional well-being and take care of themselves. They have created a fine balance between face-to-face and remote working which allows them to achieve their full potential and goals. They also have time for their families and hobbies.

Many of my clients have identified themselves within these categories, in some cases pointing out that their method of working can vary or switch from one category to another depending on the specific period or even their mood. In other words, they define themselves as *situational professionals.*

I spent a long time in the second group, I was willing but unfocused. I spent far too long, years even, in this state until I had an extreme burnout. As I set about reinventing myself professionally, I realized that first I had to become more honest and humble to understand that my way of working wasn't working. How hard it is to acknowledge what we're doing badly without making excuses! Once I became aware of the problem, I got to work to solve it and was able to join the fifth group: productive and astute. The most positive aspect is that, as well as achieving good results, I am increasingly spending more time on what really makes me happy, both professionally and personally. Have confidence in yourself and your ability: if I can do it, you can too!

Now it's your turn to reflect on the style of working that predominates in your day to day. This needs to be done with honesty and humility, without falling into self-deception.

Many people find it difficult to self-analyse in this way, so I would suggest the following five exercises:

- Make a plan of all the activities that you do every week which is where you will be able to see whether there are any activities that are not adding any value to your life and that are not truly important.
- Spot your timerobbers and bad habits in your style of work.
- Analyze your capacity to work fully focused and how long you can do it for.
- Think about how you maintain your level of energy every day, how this evolves over the course of the week, and how you feel on Fridays at the end of the week.
- Look at whether a combination of remote and office-based working might be possible, which hybrid model works best for you and the benefits it could bring, as well as minimizing any risks that could have a negative impact on your work.

From here on, this will help you to become aware of your energy levels when it comes to working. That is to say, if you are able to maintain a good level of energy throughout the day- of often waste a lot of time because of bad habits and timerobbers-and if you manage to work with full attention on the really important questions.

If you are working remotely on some days, you should also make a point of analysing how this affects your energy, what are your timerobbers and bad habits, and definitely your productivity. In addition, to avoid self-deception, it would be a good idea to ask those around you their opinion on your way of working, whilst making sure these people are the sensible and honest type,

Using the following steps of the FASE method, you will gradually work towards joining the last category, astute and productive, whether you work remotely, from the office or a mix of the two (hybrid).

> "One of the best –and least considered– ways to increase your productivity is spending time with productive people."
> **THANH PHAM**

3. The FASE method in detail

"Success is not achieved only with unique qualities.
It is, above all, a work of perseverance, method and organization."
J. P Sergent

How about you? Are you efficient?

Before you go on the journey learn more about the FASE method, you will need to really understand what a realistic goal of your working day should be. The fact is that the vast majority of people believe that they are working too many hours, mainly due to two reasons: On one hand, we tend to over- exaggerate facts and on the other hand, we are prone to include the time we spend travelling or eating in our estimates. In addition, the time we are not spending actually working, but instead doing other things that are part of our daily routines, ends up also affecting the quality of our focus and attention. Two very good examples of this can be:

1. Compulsively checking our emails – which tend to be a mix of important and more trivial issues, such as newsletters and LinkedIn alerts, that distract us from our priority tasks.
2. Checking WhatsApp messages or social media that typically relate to personal matters and leisure.

This amounts to wasting many minutes of our day, in both dealing with issues that are actually irrelevant as well as the cost of compulsively switching between multiple activities. When an executive is not willing to acknowledge this problem, I encourage them to do some self-observation for a week, record how they use their time and report back to me the end of that week. They will usually call halfway through the week to admit that I was right after all. Many people unwittingly weave their personal lives into their professional lives, which is not the result of new remote working arrangements; it is a longstanding issue. During our working day, we are dealing with too many personal matters and consequently, work ends up encroaching upon our personal time. This is something that we have been doing unintentionally and when you think about it, it actually doesn't make sense. We should try to establish clear lines between our hours of work and rest, regardless of what kind of environment you may be working in. I have clients who have made an effort and were able to achieve a balance, increasing both the quality of their work and their energy, while at the same time reclaiming a sense of harmony in their personal lives.

Implementing the FASE method will help you achieve efficiency in the sense that the hours you spend working will be real hours and not the sum of numerous interruptions to your work. You will achieve this by completing exercises that will make it easier for you to carry out the tasks you need to complete in a shorter space of time, without distractions. However, you should remember it's not only a matter of being more efficient, but also about being more effective. This means that the time you use efficiently also needs to be focused on the relevant and important tasks. And that is how you will get the results you want without having to work more hours or at a faster pace. Lastly, don't forget to keep your energy levels up throughout your working day to avoid an afternoon slump that may affect your concentration or the quality of your work.

This is the first valuable lesson of the method: it is not about working excessive hours, caught up in whatever the day throws at us, it is about working eight hours a day at maximum effectiveness. These days that turn into weeks, that turn into months are the sum total of all the tasks that you have accomplished. You will become the kind of professional who works proactively to influence your own performance and you will exceed within your area of responsibility and be well-prepared for your next professional challenges. The results after two months are truly spectacular and the sense of achievement and control will reinforce and continue to fuel this way of working.

Remember the "four Hs", the attributes you need to start improving your productivity? Well, it is now, at the beginning of this process, that you have the chance to test how honest you are with yourself, so try to be sincere as you evaluate your current way of working.

The importance of the initial self-assessment

Just as we are advised to carry out a vehicle safety inspection before setting off on a long journey if we want to plan and organize our lives, we need to start by evaluating our abilities based on the four components of the FASE method:

- **Focus:** you must be clear on what the really important tasks are (Key Important tasks or KIT) and what you need to focus on.
- **Attention:** dedicate your full attention during a limited time, without distractions.
- **Systematization:** create habits that reinforce a way of working with the logic of the method.
- **Energy:** your energy level will depend on several factors, and you will need optimum energy throughout the day.

In short, the phases that you will need to go through to implement the FASE method are:

- Undertake a self-knowledge exercise to determine your

starting point, identifying your current way of working in terms of efficiency and effectiveness.
- Understand the theory behind the method.
- Carry out the self-assessment in three parts: energy, focus and attention.
- Do the necessary exercises and rectify plans to establish a solid foundation.
- Create a framework of goals that will cascade from every month to every week, and from every week to every day, thus systematizing a series of rituals and habits.
- Carry out daily and weekly evaluations on how well you are following the method.
- Review and update your table of monthly objectives every month as a starting point.

At this point, I want to make sure you're still motivated by this process, so I'd like to remind you of the three main reasons why, by adopting this method, you will be able to better manage your professional life and achieve well-being and happiness.

- You will accomplish better results at work because you will achieve exceed in your area of responsibility.
- You will increase the amount and quality of your free time because you will be able to spend it on personal activities that make you feel good.
- You will reduce stress and gain more control over your professional life.

In addition, after four years of implementing this method, I can say with confidence that it works for people from any professional background: entrepreneurs, executives, Michelin-starred chefs, lawyers, dentists, architects, students, etc.

Focus

"Stop managing your time and start managing
where you put your focus."
ROBIN SHARMA

Timerobbers, bad habits, and tasks with no added value

To focus on what really matters and gain back hours in our day, we need to identify everything that is causing us to waste time.

In this initial phase of the method, you will need to complete two essential exercises:

1. Eliminate distractions and bad habits

- A *timerobber* is anything external that saps our time without adding value to our objectives. For example, a colleague at the office who interrupts us continually instead of making a list of issues to address at the appropriate time. Or a pet at home that demands constant attention on the days we are working remotely.

- A *bad habit* is a specific behaviour that takes up time or diminishes the effectiveness of what we do, for example, checking emails every ten minutes and our phones every three minutes. Or even watching a Netflix series in the middle of your working day.

Time robbers and bad habits are so incredibly common that I will suggest some ideas that I have successfully implemented and that have helped many others to gain back 25 % of their time every day. This involves counteracting what I call the "six enemies": email, WhatsApp, social media, internet, meetings, phone conversations and colleagues or managers who are habitual 'interrupters'. When you are working from home, the types of timerobbers and bad habits may vary, but there are still many pitfalls to watch out for. In the final section of this book, we will take a closer look at how to overcome them.

2. Delegate tasks that don't add any value

With this method, in order to rid yourself of distractions and bad habits, you need to observe your behaviours for a week to identify them, and we would then work on changing and eliminating them. Once you have identified your timerobbers, you have to draw up a plan or mind map to include all the tasks that you are currently working on. In most cases, thanks to the first self-observation exercise, you should be able to determine which tasks have no added value so that you can either delegate them or remove them from your routine, helping you to gain hours back every week. However, many people soon realize that they actually classified all tasks as urgent, but they didn't focus on what was really important- what brings you results. When you have managed to identify what you need to do to stop wasting time, you will also need to draft a plan to establish which issues and activities are actually important and invest your time accordingly.

> "Each activity you engage in has a cost of chance. Instead of focusing on being more efficient, invest time. Reflecting on what tasks and activities you should eliminate from your life."
>
> **GREG MCKEOWN**

Objectives and Most Important Tasks (MITs)

- An *objective* is something you need to achieve in your role at work, area of responsibility or even your personal life. Objectives can vary in nature, from leading a team to launching a project within the deadline or running a half marathon. It could be a specific project with an end date, or other ongoing objectives that form part of your day-to-day responsibilities.
- A *Most Important Task* is an activity or action that you need to carry out, periodically or otherwise, to make progress in achieving your objectives It might be useful to make a note of people that could be involved in your MITs in case you need their help or input.

> "The essence of self-discipline is to do the important thing rather than the urgent thing."
> **BARRY WERNER**

To stay focused, I would recommend typing up the essential objectives that you want to achieve in an Excel spreadsheet, along with the tasks that you will need to complete to successfully achieve each objective. You will need to focus your full attention on these key MITs. I also recommend classifying your objectives in order of importance, defining them well so that they are concrete and measurable, and setting yourself a deadline to achieve them. For example: "attract two new clients every month".

You will also need to review these objectives on a monthly basis to monitor which ones you have achieved, whether there are any that you need to spend more time on, or whether your priority objectives have shifted. Some objectives cease to exist once they have been achieved, others may no longer be relevant while others may gain or lose importance.

EXAMPLE. OBJECTIVE: TO BECOME A UNIVERSITY LECTURER

HIT 1: Obtain my doctorate.

HIT 2: Attain the required level of English to teach in the language.

HIT 3: Speak to people in academia and ask for their guidance.

HIT 4: Consider which areas I have the most experience in, to be able to teach classes and prepare course materials.

Each objective will involve a different number of MITs. I have encountered people who, after carrying out this exercise, can immediately spot how little time they have been dedicating to their key priority objectives and corresponding tasks until then.

Fight procrastination

Even after committing to a plan to stick to your objectives and MITs , we might still have to come face to face with a powerful enemy: procrastination. Procrastination, also known as "active laziness", involves postponing important tasks and substituting them with other simpler or more pleasurable activities. Procrastinators tend to work on what they feel like doing and not what they should be working on or they tackle the easiest task instead of the most complex one.

Much has been written on this theme, but I want to highlight the opinion of the psychologist Neil Fiore.[12] He believes that procrastination is a coping mechanism, used to deal with the anxiety associated when starting or completing some tasks. It is important to bear this in mind because we will, on occasion, find ourselves trying not to avoid dealing with the very important tasks that we have clearly identified. Delaying these tasks is nothing more than a defence or avoidance mechanism and while it may offer

12. Neil Fiore, *Now Habit: A Strategic Program for Overcoming Procrastination and Enjoying Guilt-free Play* (Jeremy P Tarcher, 2007)

immediate gratification by reducing the internal tension, in the medium term there will be far worse consequences.

In the face of this active laziness that hijacks (almost) all us of us when we need to complete important tasks, I use very simple but effective solutions such as:

- Thinking about the pleasure I feel by not postponing things, as opposed to the annoyance I feel when fall behind with something.
- Rewarding myself with a treat if I make progress in a complex issue.
- Tackling the MITs first thing in the morning when I have more energy and work on less complex tasks at the end of the day.

Making a start by setting myself a very modest goal. The simple act of beginning something always delivers more than expected, like in the exercise, in Stephen Guise's book. on how to undertake a daily reflection to acquire a new habit.[13]

Urgent tasks (UTs) and other pending tasks

In addition to the MITs, there are other less important tasks that will gain importance as the deadline approaches and

13. Stephen Guise, *Mini Habits: Smaller Habits, Bigger Results* (Wisdom Tree Publications, 2020)

will need to be completed within a set timeframe. These can be defined as urgent tasks (UTs). A typical UT could be buying a train ticket or organizing files and correspondence on our desk. Completing an MIT requires a lot more effort and cognitive skill than that needed for a UT.

There are also other pending tasks that will start turning into UTs as the deadline approaches and it is a good idea to have a system to record them. To get organized, you need to bear in mind that new things will always crop up and you will need to be able to keep track of them. I recommend recording these items immediately in one of the two categories of tasks: MITs and remaining tasks that will become UTs. I also advise recording them electronically, on Outlook for example, because the notifications and alerts will make it easier to keep track of them (even though paper diaries seem to be making a come back). In addition, relying solely on your memory, may potentially let you down and trying to memorize pending tasks can consume the energy you need for other activities, such as problem-solving.

As my clients start embedding the method into their projects, they also send me their observations and feedback form which I never stop learning and that also enrich the method. One client differentiated between MITs and UTs by saying that "MITs were for the commute on the train into work first thing in the morning when your mind is fresh mind and UTs were for the commute home at night when you have less energy". Another client pointed out that some UTs, as the deadline approaches, end up becoming, as he phrased it, "MIT-UT", in other words, very important issues that are also urgent, such as responding to an important client's complaint. And with the arrival of remote working, some of my clients have decided to make the most of working from home to spend more time on their MITs. This is another one of the great benefits of combining remote working with working from the office. Not only do we gain time when we no longer need to commute, but we also have greater control over our capacity to work with full attention on the Most Important Tasks with the time we have gained.

More is not better

The Pareto principle – also known as the 20/80 rule – was first articulated by the eminent Italian sociologist and economist Vilfredo Pareto at the beginning of the twentieth century when he noted that 20 % of the population owned 80 % of the country's land or wealth, in contrast to the 80 % who owned only 20 %. This principle also extended to politics and economics and today, it can also be applied to productivity. In this field, we refer to the Pareto principle to demonstrate that 20 % of the most important tasks that we carry out can yield 80 % of our results.

That is to say, by dedicating time to this 20 % of issues or relevant projects (I like to call them *big rocks*)[14] you will

14. *Big rocks* refer to these important, priority tasks that we need to have top

achieve 80 % of your most significant results. For this, you will have to prioritize those really crucial tasks and dedicate quality time to them, otherwise, you run the risk of spending time on issues that are not part of the 20 % of most important tasks.

> "Most of us spend too much time on what is urgent and not enough time on what is important."
> **STEVEN COVEY**

When you do your weekly planning, it is important to have a clear idea of which MITs and UTs you want to work on the following week. You then, need to review them daily and organize them in terms of priority:

- Firstly, the MIts, which move you closer to achieving your objectives and, as such, are of vital importance. For example, preparing for an annual meeting with a client to plan the next quarter.
- Secondly, the UTs-they are the less important tasks but come with an "expiry date", hence the pressing need to complete them. For example, making a travel reservation for a business trip the following week.

---

of mind and written down to make it easier for us to spend time on them. They are the crucial MITs at any given point and it's a good idea to review them every month.

And finally, the other less important tasks or issues that are not urgent but as time passes, usually turn into UTs. For example, considering which trade fairs to attend the following year.

The first part, setting objectives and assigning the tasks that will lead you towards achieving them, is one of the cornerstones or pillars of the method, and illustrates the difference between being always busy working on something and being focused on the most productive and essential tasks. Planning involves a great deal of self-discipline for two reasons: on one hand, it requires a considerable personal effort to focus on the most essential matters and not on what you feel like doing. And on the other hand, it involves learning how to say no to others when their requests lead you away from of your daily mission to work on your MITs.

One of the first things I do with the executives I mentor, is to ascertain whether they are really dedicating time to work on the essential tasks that will bring them results as this is more important than the number of hours they work.

As the business management expert Tom Peters says:

We have all had days when we get carried away trying to tackle everything that falls into our in-tray. Days spent answering emails, going to meetings, answering the phone, and completing simple tasks. In the end, you feel like you have worked intensely but you haven't managed to achieve anything important or that you haven't spent your time wisely. This is something that will inevitably weigh on your mind and lead to stress.

However, some of my clients confess that it is actually comfortable for them to work on autopilot. But *intensity* is not the same as *efficiency*. The problem is that when this turns into a routine, you will never dedicate quality time to really crucial matters, or even take a step back to think and assess, which means that your results will never be what you desired. The results from executives who work fewer hours, but are focused on what really matters, are greater than those who work intensely but not what they should be working on We often confuse business with effectiveness.

Personally, I must admit that for many of my years as an executive, I worked obsessively but chaotically, that is to say, I would work fourteen hours a day but in a disastrous way. I tried to make up for a lack of system and order by increasing the hours of work each day. I took on ever more tasks, many of which made no sense. I was drowning in bad habits and timerobbers. My diet was terrible, I did no exercise, I was overweight and my personal life was increasingly impacted by the chronic stress I was suffering. Over time, I realised that there is no more powerful ritual than thinking at the end of every day about the MITs that you have tackled that day and the ones that you will tackle the next day. Some days there will be exceptional circumstances that will force you to readjust your planning, but it is precisely with this final exercise that you will be able to get back on track the following day, so that nothing can get in the way of your MITs.

Learn to say "no"

Being able to say "no" is one the skills I really struggled with since there are some people who seem to be experts at making you feel bad, when you say no. The personal productivity experts that I have met are very skilled at saying no without causing conflict. A simple technique is to communicate clearly so that others will understand your reasons and then promise to help them in the future. At times, being productive demands courage and putting boundaries in place.

Schedule your MIT sessions

Once you have identified the essential tasks to achieve your objectives and incorporated them on a daily and weekly basis- and experienced the feeling of satisfaction at having met your goals at the end of the weekly-you will need to create a series of habits. These will ensure that, once a week, you take time to reflect both on the tasks that you need to complete, and the time that you will dedicate to them each day.

Let's look at these habits:

- A weekly reflection on the MITs to plan for the following week by also highlighting those that we tend to postpone due to fear of failure and ensuring that these are placed side by side with your objectives MITs and your schedule planning.,

- Start each day by selecting the MIT that you want to work on that day, although some people prefer to do it the bay before which is also ok.
- In order to really deal with your MITs face on and with the right frequency, you should ensure you have blocked some time on your schedule when you can work fully focused and without interruptions. I call these '45-minute MIT sessions'. They are 45 minute time slots which I like to describe as 'having a meeting with yourself'. I would recommend making sure that these time slots are 'visually present', as research has shown that you are more likely to complete a task if you can actually see it in your diary. Some companies even go as far as sharing the same '45-minute session' slots with the team, to ensure that everyone actually uses this time accordingly. Personally, I like to do it first thing in the morning and before and after lunch.
- The idea is to have two (three would be optimum) blocks of time every day to work on your assigned MITs. After each 45-minute slot, you have ten minutes to check your email or your phone and then five minutes to rest. My one-hour blocks usually look like this:
- 45 minutes giving my full attention to a HIT with no distractions.
- 10 minutes checking and answering emails, urgent calls or WhatsApp messages.

- Five minutes of restorative time, going for a short walk or having a quiet.

In these 45-minute HIT sessions, I have a ritual that helps me to achieve maximum concentration:

1. Let those around me know (wherever possible) that I will be doing concentrated work. I do this in the office and also when I work remotely so that people at home are aware.
2. Find a space where I can be alone or shut the door of the office I'm in.
3. Set the objective or HIT to work on during this period of time.
4. Set an alarm on my phone for 45 minutes.
5. Enable airplane mode on my phone and keep it out of sight.
6. Turn off the wifi.

The reason for steps 3-6 is that experience has taught me that if you are not really strict about banishing your phone and access to email, it is highly likely that you will want to check them because we are often seeking that emotional incentive.

You can make the most of the five- and ten-minute restorative periods to rest at key points throughout the day, go for a walk to stretch your legs and clear your head after lunch or take a 20-minute power nap. This practice is very common in Asian cultures. I also want to emphasize that these periods of rest are physiologically necessary for us to sustain periods of concentration and maximum productivity which creates a sense of flow. The term flow was first coined by Mihály Csíkszentmihályi[15] in reference to this state of maximum concentration that enables you to reach levels of proactivity and creativity that exceed your own expectations and during which your mind functions at peak performance. When you enter into a state of flow in your MIT sessions, you will achieve a level of concentration that will improve the quality of your work and improve your efficiency, making complex tasks seem much more manageable.

It is so very important not to make the mistake of spending these 45 minute slots on UTs. Let's just recap the big difference between MITs and UTs : the MITs are the important tasks that also require concentration and involve complexity, while the UTs are tasks that are simple or repetitive, but they have deadlines that must be taken into consideration. , It is much better to spend time on UTs when you start to feel exhausted and that your capabilities are waning. This helps to make use of less productive time to get things done and replenish your energy for the next MIT session. I recommend spending time on UTs at the end of the day when tiredness starts to set in, or straight after lunch.

Personally, I like to schedule the highly complex tasks that require greater attention for the early morning and I

15. A professor of psychology at the University of Claremont is credited with developing the concept of flow.

leave the more mechanical and less demanding tasks such as answering emails and completing for the afternoon. I also try to help the people I work closest with to see that this system works for me and that it would also be good for them to implement it.

This first step of defining our priority objectives and their corresponding MITs as well as differentiating them from other pending tasks is key to starting this new focused way of working. All professionals have a range of different activities as part of their day to day: meetings, conferences, work lunches, reading correspondence or checking emails. This is why it is essential that you ensure you have slotted your 45-minute HIT sessions into your diary. This system, will allow you to have 2 things: on one hand, you will have a table with your objectives and HITs, which you will review monthly. On the other hand, you will also have a record of the outstanding tasks that will become UTs as their deadlines approach. This way, you will have identified what you need to be dedicating your time to every day and every week, as well as being as being able to differentiate which tasks or activities are much more important regardless of their urgency.

> "Use your time like your money. When you have little money, you spend it according to the highest priority for your well-being. In the same way, allocate your time to tasks based on what get you closer to reaching your goals."
>
> **DAN ARIELY**

With these daily HIT sessions, you will be able to invest time in the most important issues, identify when you haven't done this and, as a result, understand why you haven't achieved your objectives. This ongoing process of consistent reflection generates a truly constructive commitment to yourself. Classifying objectives, as well as assigning tasks, should be led by the importance of completing each one. Remember that to achieve objectives and successful results it is essential to dedicate your full attention to the most crucial tasks.

Make the most of the moments when you can group together tasks of the same nature

Planning your schedule so that you can group together tasks of the same nature might not be everyone's idea of fun, but it is highly beneficial for your life. If you know which similar tasks to accumulate for particular blocks of time, it is much easier to complete them automatically, without allowing them to interfere with other tasks, thus gaining productivity. Just as you schedule time for important and urgent tasks, it is also good to create slots for these grouped together tasks, to check and return phone calls and answer messages or emails. It makes sense to schedule these tasks for the down time between one activity and another, while you have a coffee or move from one space to another, which also brings a gratifying sense of progress and achievement.

Attention

"The ability to work with mindfulness is becoming increasingly rare,
but, at the same time, it is increasingly valued.
Those who cultivate it and bet on it will succeed."

CAL NEWPORT

One of the most important aspects of the FASE method is working with full attention, fully engaged in a single task for the duration of time needed to complete it, or at least enough time to make progress on it. Compared to the stress of multitasking, working with full attention on one single activity induces a feeling of achievement and elicits positive emotions. This is why you should bring your full attention, free from distractions, to all the tasks in your day that require so, such as HIT sessions and one to one meetings. At the same time, you should be doing your best to avoid multitasking so that it gradually starts to disappear from your style of working.

Multitasking is not in human nature

These days we never seem to be able to stay focused enough to complete one task in a set amount of time. This is such a big problem, that it has been recognized by business experts. We are trying to be as thorough as possible when completing complex tasks- such as an annual plan, negotiation or conflict resolutions- but we end up only being able to do them in 5 or 10 minutes blocks or stopping and starting again, and again, because of constant interruptions or distractions. This is the technique that most of the professionals tend to use these days, instead of being able to focus on these relevant tasks, consistently, for, say 45 uninterrupted minutes of fully engaged work.

I have encountered many people who try to convince me that multitasking works well and is productive for them. But multitasking does not mean, as many people believe, the ability to do many different things at the same time. Instead, it is a process that involves carrying out a sequence of activities, switching from one to the next in rapid succession. As such, multitasking does not exist at all because there is always a short period of time between swapping from one activity to another and the corresponding time that it takes to kickstart the next task. Ultimately, it is a practice that results in a completely illogical process of starting one task, switching to a different task only to return to the initial task before the cycle repeats. It is estimated that 40 % of productivity is lost when we try to do two or more things at once. This also leads to more negative impacts, such as an increase in stress and impaired memory. We should also be aware of the image that we are projecting to others when we are apparently listening to them but at the same time reading a message on our phone. And it is for all these reasons that it is important to schedule two MIT sessions a day.

Any project or task with a degree of complexity needs to be completed with the following two requisites in mind:

- Work on these complex and relevant tasks in blocks of 45 minutes of uninterrupted time. In my experience, this is the ideal amount of time that allows for the intensity of concentration without having to neglect other responsibilities.
- Work on these projects regularly, for example, two or three times a week. This way, you have a much better chance of establishing a good progression plan as opposed to cramming two days into the project before the deadline and expecting a good result.

IWhen there is an approach to work that allows for continuous interruptions or jumping from one activity to another, the quality of our work will never reach its potential. There is no easy solution to this problem and in all probability, it is one of the most complex challenges we face when changing our working style in search of greater productivity.

The reason for this struggle is more a matter of human nature that is important to highlight here: the executive part of the brain, the prefrontal cortex, and the emotional part of the brain, the limbic system, are in competition. The first deals with reason, logic and what is appropriate for the situation, while the second relates to emotion. The prefrontal cortex regulates what we should do, the limbic system governs what we want to do or what feels comfortable. Because of this, it can be hard to resist some temptations, such as the internet, or a simple enjoyable chat with a colleague instead of staying focused on a project for a specific period of time. The limbic system is constantly seeking out new stimuli and novelty, so considerable effort is needed to keep this in check. We mustn't also forget what was mentioned earlier with regards to procrastination, which also leads us to focus on less important tasks in order to avoid tackling issues that might be less appealing or more complex.

Once you become aware of this, you will be able to start fixing it (after a significant initial effort) and you will start to work on your MITs with full attention, and in turn, strengthen the pre-frontal cortex with activities that stretch our capacity for attention and reflection. As well as enhancing the quality of work, you will also notice that your memory improves, along with your energy throughout the day. The alternative of multitasking, as well as being unproductive, leaves you feeling drained because your pre-frontal cortex is in a constant state of chaos. You need to bear in mind that full attention is like a muscle that needs to be exercised daily in order to develop and, in many cases, it is a muscle that has atrophied due to the current excess multitasking, hyperconnectivity and over-stimulation. To recover this muscle elasticity, you should look into activities such as reading, writing, memory and concentration exercises such as crosswords and sudokus, learning a foreign language as well as practising yoga or Pilates can help. II have often observed that, in my clients, there seems to be a correlation between their capacity for concentration and having hobbies that demand prolonged attention for a certain amount of time.

To gradually develop the capacity to fully work in blocks of time on the really important issues, I recommend following the "2 x 45 min rule": this is about having at least two 45-minute sessions of maximum concentration each day (preferably three). Initially, it may be extremely difficult to concentrate on one single task, as this is an ability that most of us have lost over time. On the other hand, if you can harness your willpower and self-control to gradually increase the amount of time, these HIT sessions will increase in quality and quantity. It is the same as when you take up jogging, every time you do it, you somehow manage to increase your capacity to keep running for longer.

Make a conscious effort to distance yourself from distractions and dedicate this time to the MIT sessions that you have planned for that week and that day. It is also important to let others know when you will be using these time slots, even using a symbol or signal for this purpose so that it is clear to all. Some people choose to work in a space (their "sanctuary") where they are less likely to be interrupted, two or three times a day, to achieve their 45-minute stretch of full attention.

A minority of my clients prefer 60 or 90 minutes of maximum concentration, but this is more difficult to achieve because we have other tasks to attend to throughout the day that also need to be factored in, and our attention tends to wane after 45 minutes. It has been demonstrated scientifically that spending more than 90 minutes on the same task without a break is difficult. A short, ten-minute restorative break, such as a relaxing activity or a walk, is required.

Remember that if you want to be productive, you have to concentrate on one thing at a time. I know that new technologies offer tempting distractions and that open-plan offices encourage continuous interruptions from work colleagues, but I can assure you that truly productive people do not multitask, as the productivity expert Julie Morgenstern rightly points out.[16]

As strange as this may seem, the capacity to concentrate on a single task for more than thirty minutes at a time has become a stand-out ability among professionals, provided that this attention is dedicated to the most important tasks (MITs). The quality of reflections and productivity that is achieved in these periods of maximum attention are the same attributes that lead the way for big ideas and solutions.

16. Julie Morgenstern, *Organizing From the Inside Out* (Owl Books, 2004).

I had to make a great effort to rectify these tendencies in myself and eliminate inefficient working practices. Now that I have achieved this, any time I slip back into multitasking, I always find that my work ends up being of poorer quality, and I tend to be more stressed and exhausted at the end of the day.

I always encourage my clients to observe themselves over the course of a day to take note of their longest period of sustained full attention. The results can be as spectacular as they are depressing. My advice is always the same: avoid temptation, people who distract you and limit access to email, phone as well as the internet. You may well need to shut yourself away either in a meeting room or close the office door and keep your electronic devices at a distance (a very simple and effective technique is to keep your phone out of sight, that way you aren't tempted to reach for it). Gradually, you will increase the amount of time you spend working with deeper concentration, just as you did when you had to study hard for your exams.

The arrival of a hybrid working model, combining remote and office-based working, has led to a new way of thinking in this area. Many people are investing the time they have gained back from the daily commute into MIT sessions, something that was often difficult to do in offices due to background noise and interruptions. Others, by contrast, have confessed to multitasking, such as answering emails, checking their phone and browsing the internet during their online meetings. We need to be more aware of the harmful effect that this practice can create, both at an individual and group level.

My concentration aids

Cultivating a reading habit is something I would highly recommend, regardless of the genre that you choose. In my case, my personal and professional interest has led me to read many personal development books and, despite the bad press they seem to get in certain sectors of society, many of these books have been really useful. Another genre that encourages growth is the biographies written about successful people. Reading has many positive effects, but I would like to highlight two: not only do we learn but we also develop our attention span, comprehension and retention, which are essential for cognitive development.

Some additional tips would include:

- Taking notes in meetings or training sessions.
- Drafting plans or mind maps before every meeting.
- Drafting a plan or mind map of complex topics to address.
- Writing down your reflections at the end of the day about all that went well or anything that could have gone better.
- Listening to podcasts or watching videos, taking note of any useful learning.

And of course, bearing in mind how much our emotional

wellbeing influences our abilities, you need to try to achieve your best emotional state possible every day. We will address this topic in more depth later in the book, but here are some pointers:

- Using positive language and avoiding extremely negative thinking. This may seem surprising, but it can truly influence concentration.
- Maintaining positive body language and gestures, for example avoiding hunching your shoulders, having a downcast facial expression or crossing your arms.
- Limiting negative thoughts that can deplete your capacities and eat into valuable time.
- Intentionally avoiding toxic people, whoever they may be.
- Exercising for at least thirty minutes a day.
- Reading about and deepening your knowledge of the wide field of emotional intelligence.
- Observing and learning from people who are emotionally stable.

Applying these and other habits requires an initial investment in energy, willpower, and discipline until they become part of your routines. This is not something that can be implemented overnight, nor is it simple to convert these behaviours into everyday practices. But you need to overcome the mental barrier that often stops us from kickstarting these strategies, and instead, you should think about all the positive benefits they will bring. And above all, in the face of difficulty, you have to make the effort every day to initiate these new activities that you want to turn into habits. Simply by starting an activity makes it easier for you to continue, more than you might think. For example, taking up exercise again after years of inactivity can start with just one stretch. This reduces resistance and, invariably, once you have done one stretch, you will be able to do more. And gradually, every day, the number of stretches increases. Productive habits function in the same way and in the coming chapters we will focus on how to create them.

The law of 1 % marginal gains

There are sometimes projects of such complexity, requiring so much time (I call them "super MITs"), that just thinking about everything that needs to be done can cause anxiety and paralyze us. So, day after day, we put off making a start.

Dave Brailsford, a British cycling coach and the creator of a training program that elevated the performance of British cycling to new heights, uses the concept of *marginal gains* to refer to the gradual improvement that takes place when we dedicate a little bit of time to a project every day. According to Brailsford, this consistency could lead to a minimum improvement of 1 % every day.

Therefore, any project that you dedicate 30 minutes to every day will yield spectacular progress in just a few weeks. Time has shown me that daily or weekly frequency is much more important than the amount of time you dedicate to doing something. Frequency and consistency are much more effective than an overload of time and effort. The "little bit by little every day" always triumphs over doing two days of intense cramming on a project. In addition to progressing in your project, you will also improve your capacity to work with full attention and develop habits and behaviours that many people have lost.

> "It's not the big things that add up in the end; it's the hundreds, thousands, or millions of little things that separate the ordinary from the extraordinary."
>
> **DARREN HARDY**

As I mentioned before my greatest challenge in terms of having enough concentration and discipline was in trying to obtain my doctorate. I decided to dedicate the first hour of the day to planning how to improve these areas over a period of months. It became my first cognitive activity in the morning, and it allowed me to advance at greater speed leading to a good end result. I still apply this strategy now to many other challenges and projects and by doing this for 45 minutes only a day, I can still achieve significant progress.

Circadian rhythms

This concept is important both when referring to weeks as well as the rhythm of our day to day lives. Everyone has certain times of the day or days of the week when they are more productive because that is in human nature. According to these circadian cycles, there are times of the day when we perform better, while at other times, we feel depleted, sluggish and lacking in motivation, states that can have a strong influence on the quality of our work. We can call the time of day when we can produce our best work because we feel good the "Optimum time of the day"- OTD.

Over the course of your working day, observe which times of the day you find yourself more capable to perform due to increased energy and concentration levels. You should then make this the time when you work on your most important tasks or the most complex issues. This is what Brian Tracy popularized with his famous quote "eat that frog first". There are people who work better first thing in the morning – the early birds – and others who find their best moment of the day once the first hours have passed or those who perform better in the evening – the night owls. Obviously, the most complex and important tasks need to be in line with your circadian cycle and they must be assigned to these OTD. This is the case not only with cognitive energy but also with physical energy when exercising. Our bodies are naturally more prepared for exercise in the afternoons as opposed to early in the morning, as the neuroscientist and researcher Orfeu Buxton notes in his study on the ideal metabolism for sport. Nevertheless, each person has their own natural rhythms and different circadian cycles. It is about observing yourself and how you respond to the different cycles and allocating your MITs (in work as well as in doing exercise) to the best times of the day for you when your energy levels are at their peak.

This is also relevant when you take the week as a whole: people tend to be more productive on Tuesdays, Wednesdays and Thursdays, while Mondays and Fridays are often less so.[17] Therefore, it makes sense to leave the less complex issues for Mondays and Fridays and address the most important tasks in the middle of the week. However, this varies from person to person, so it is important to discover what your natural rhythms are when creating your new habits.

With the increasing possibilities of combining remote working with office-based working, many people have been able to ascertain which days are best suited to working at the office and which are best suited to working from home, as well as which types of activities are appropriate for each case. Many people are increasing their number of MIT sessions on the days they work from home while saving meetings and other activities in which their presence brings an added value for their office-based days.

17. Research conducted at the Clinical Research Centre of the University of Chicago.

Systematization

> "The key is not to prioritize what's on your schedule, but to schedule your priorities."
> **STEVEN COVEY**

Systematizing is about creating daily, weekly and monthly habits and routines that are key to achieving maximum productivity and effectiveness, both personally and professionally. This involves embedding good practices into regular routines that will go on to become ingrained habits and therefore automatically become part of your way of working. For example, my habit of planning my week on Sunday evenings is so ingrained that it no longer requires any effort.

In the initial phase of a process to improve productivity, we need to unlearn the bad habits that have taken root before we can create new ones, and this involves considerable effort. Once we have eliminated the bad habits, we will need to create new ones and gradually substitute unhelpful practices with effective ones. We cannot, nor should we try to, integrate too many new habits within a short space of time as this would require a lot of energy and willpower, something that usually depletes as the day goes on. On the other hand, once we manage to repeat good practices regularly, they will start to become embedded as routines and this will free us up to tackle new challenges. As you begin to instil new habits that become grounded in routines, you will save a lot of energy throughout the day because the fatigue of having to think and make decisions is reduced. It's a bit like being on autopilot but in a good way, going in the right direction. When the demands of the FASE model become part of your daily routine it is clear to see that the method has been successfully embedded. There is a true sense of satisfaction that I share with clients once they have managed to achieve this.

Carrying out these habits and behaviours with the necessary regularity will improve your productivity. At the same time, it will help you to sustain these disciplined practices over an extended period of time.

The main habits that we need to create as part of the FASE method are:

- Every month, review and update your table of objectives, MITs and monthly *big rocks*.
- On a weekly basis, draft a plan for the week.
- Every day, draft the daily plan (the day before).

- At the start of every day, review the plan for the day, and schedule at least two (preferably three) MIT sessions of full attention.
- Schedule in time to group activities together: reading and responding to emails, messages or calls to be made.
- At the end of each today: have a moment of reflection (which should coincide with planning the following day).

The habit of drafting the weekly plan

Creating this habit involves dedicating a maximum of one hour to structuring and planning the week according to the FASE method. There are those who do this planning on Friday afternoons, others on Sundays, and some on Monday mornings as the first task of the week. I wouldn't recommend this last option because if any unforeseen circumstances should arise on a Monday, you may find yourself starting the week without a plan.

The process is always the same:

- Reflecting on the achievements of the previous week with an attitude of constructive self-criticism, on how well organized you have been and the objectives you have met.
- Visualizing appointments and meetings while drafting your schedule.
- Factoring in two (preferably three) MIT sessions daily, depending on how your week is shaping up.

- Making a list of MITs for the week (you will find them in the Excel spreadsheet "Objectives, MITs and "*big rocks*".
- Reviewing your UTs of the week (you will find them in your Outlook to-do list, bearing in mind their deadlines which will turn these pending tasks into UTs).

It is also important to consider which days you will work from the office and which days you will work from home, if this is an option for you, as it will obviously have a bearing on your planning when assigning each day's activities for the following week.

- Planning for Monday as the first day of the week.

Planning your week is a very useful way of improving your focus and thinking about which aspects you want to improve over the course of the week. With this snapshot of the week, the next step is to zoom in at the end of each day to plan the following day. As driving instructors never tired of reminding us, we mustn't forget to adjust our rear-view mirror, which, in planning terms, means reviewing the completion of our MITs and UTs from the previous week and assessing whether we are following the FASE method in a committed and serious manner.

> "As a professional, your playing field is your weekly calendar. A good way to tell if you're playing well is to look at the real value or the importance of each week's activities and appointments."
>
> **TODD HERMAN**

The habit of creating a daily plan

This method, like many other time management methods, requires daily self-evaluation to reaffirm what works well and correct what doesn't and, above all, to create new habits. This involves spending some time at the start of each day to see what we need to do and some time at the end of the day to assess how the day has gone and plan for the following day.

By doing the daily and weekly planning, you will have an outline or "order of business" at the start of each day, to complete your relevant objectives: the medium and long-term objectives (MIT) and those with deadlines that need to be addressed in the short term (UTs). You can also schedule the sessions to work on accumulated tasks such as checking and answering emails, making calls or dealing with work or personal messages. At the end of the day, reflect briefly on what you have done and review your schedule for the following day.

In my experience, I can often see that tasks that don't have a *when* or a *how* attached to them are rarely completed. This means that certain actions need to be ritualized so that they become habits we can really sustain. One of the routines or habits that I found most positively impacted my productivity has been the use of ten minutes of reviewing the day ahead each morning, straight after breakfast. In those first ten minutes, I look over all the meetings and activities for the day, and I schedule the blocks of time for concentrated work – I always try to factor in at least two

MIT sessions – and I review the list of weekly MIT and UT that I can make a start on, that day. Lastly, if I have an important meeting or activity scheduled, I draft a quick mind map or plan of what I want to achieve by the end of it. I have to say that this morning habit has really increased my productivity exponentially. There have also been some people that have told me that they weren't able to follow the same habit it and I always try to explain that they probably didn't keep going for long enough for the changes to cement into habits or daily rituals.

Remember that 'MIT moments' represent one of the basic cornerstones of the FASE method. To make the most of these sessions, you have to bear in mind external factors such as switching off your phone or placing it out of reach and, if necessary, informing anyone who may contact you during this time. You will also need to be aware of internal factors, in other words, the times of the day when your motivation and energy are at their peak to cultivate full attention.

Acquiring habits is the key to everything

As we have established, a habit is a routine behaviour that is repeated on a regular basis, and which eventually becomes automatic. In order to be able to adopt a new habit, we need to mobilize all our willpower and energy. The problem is that willpower and energy tend to deplete, and this can often happen before the habit has become fully integrated. Given that patterns of behaviour that we repeat often are deeply entrenched in our minds, this explains why old habits are so hard to break and new ones are so difficult to acquire.

The writer and leadership and personal development expert Robin Sharma, explains in his "Habit Installation Protocol" that "change is hard at first, messy in the middle, and gorgeous at the end". He also notes that this process can take roughly two months, going through three consecutive phases: destruction, confusion and integration.

Based on my own personal experience, this is also the timeframe that I usually recommend to others when implementing a process to improve productivity. The first stage is to eliminate the old ways of working and gradually become aware of everything that needs to change. The second stage, confusion, is when you abandon the old habits forever while integrating and systematizing the new ones. Finally, the third stage is where you complete the process of change until the new way of working becomes fully cemented.

In the second stage, once you have managed to eliminate the old habits, it is important to create a series of new positive habits following the three key concepts that I will outline later in the book. After this two-month period, you won't even have to think about these habits anymore, they will have become automatic to you. It will also be important to schedule routines to work on more complex tasks at times of the day when your energy and willpower at are their peak, leaving more mechanical and reactive tasks for when fatigue starts to creep in.

There are many other theories about what it really takes to create a new habit. In line with Robin Sharma's work, there is also a study[18] that found that acquiring a new habit takes 66 days. Yes, It takes serious effort, but the reward is immense. In only two months of your life, you can mould your behaviour which will lead to professional success and life satisfaction.

The three key moments

To successfully introduce these positive practices into our daily routines, we need to find our motivation first, something that drives us so that the effort required feels worthwhile. As there are many changes and new habits to incorporate as part of the process to improve productivity, you will need to take small gradual steps, steadily and continuously. So, it is better to start with small goals that you always complete at the same time every day. As you repeat this activity, your brain makes the necessary connections to turn this into automatic behaviour.

As I mentioned earlier in the book, when creating new habits, there are three key concepts: the trigger, the routine and the reward. It is very important for you to find a stimulus or trigger that will lead to the behaviour related to the new habit. You will then have to set a routine carrying

18. Lally, P.; Van Jaarsveld, C. H. M.: Potts, H. W. W., y Wardle, J. (2010). "How our habits are formed: Modelling habit formation in the real world", European Journal of Social Psychology, vol. 40, n.6º, pp. 998-1009.

out this behaviour at the same time and under the same circumstances every day, ideally minimizing the risk of tempting distractions that might divert you from your goal, for example, you should turn off off the Wi-Fi and keeping your phone out of sight. Finally, you should reward yourself for completing the behaviour – a technique that is frequently used in psychology to reinforce positive behaviour so that the brain can detect the activators that will bring rewards. This will make it much easier to carry out an action that will later become a habit.

For example, in my case, I'm in the habit of reviewing my daily plan and starting my first MIT session of the day while having a coffee in my kitchen. This behaviour is now so completely internalised and automatic in me, that the first sip of coffee is the trigger to start the routine or habit of reviewing the day. The reward is the music I play in the car on my way to work and this is how my subconscious has assimilated the behaviour. Some people are triggered to do the review at the end of their working day and the planning for the next day with the action of turning off their computer.

> "Change might not be fast, and it isn't always easy.
> But with time and effort, almost any habit can be reshaped."
> **CHARLES DUHIGG**

The power of discipline

When I observe people who are happy and fulfilled in their work, one common trait that seems to unite them is having the discipline to always focus on doing what is really important. And this discipline can be detected in the daily and weekly habits that are aligned with your aims, helping you to achieve them and boost concentration. And over time, these routines will form or reinforce part of your character, your identity - that of an effective person. This is precisely how I understand discipline: the capacity to create and maintain positive habits, developing rituals that make it easier for you to stick to them. Being disciplined makes it easier to achieve the desired frequency and repetition, as well as helping you to overcome the tough times, keeping your work regulated, and to go from intention to action, even when you least feel like it. Consequently, creating new habits and having the discipline to maintain them means that we won't be so reliant on willpower which, like energy, has its daily limits- and boost our confidence in our own abilities.

As I went through this process although I always knew what the next step would be, I also had to remain determined and disciplined. It can be easy to feel discouraged, and to get sidetracked for hours or work on fruitless activities when dealing with difficult or complex situations,. In my case, I fought very hard to stay disciplined and because of this, I was able to fully identify with a quote that I had read: "Routines and habits speak volumes about a person". That is to say that a disciplined person projects an image of integrity and efficiency. The key to success is having the willpower to create the habits and the discipline to maintain them. This model of discipline links back to the struggle between the executive brain and the emotional brain, between the pre-frontal cortex and the limbic system, between what we should do and what we find pleasant and easy to do.

How to make habits stick

Daily Diary

A daily diary entry isn't about writing a short story about your day, it is about making some observations on how your day has gone, the positive aspects, what you've learned or anything you may have found. noteworthy. This habit is particularly beneficial for:

- Carrying out a written self-evaluation on how your planning and organization is working, checking whether you are going in the right direction or whether there is anything you need to adjust.
- Reflecting on your progress on the main priorities.
- Expressing your emotional state, which is a good self-analysis technique and a fantastic way to put your thoughts or frame of mind into perspective, simply by writing them down.

Active mindfulness: cultivating full attention

In addition to the MIT sessions during which you are working with full attention on important issues, there are also other techniques that help you to think, come up with ideas, and find solutions to relevant issues in a more informal way. Some of my clients practice what we call "active reflection", which involves selecting an issue of some importance and spending some time thinking about it in your free time, during a car journey or while going for a walk or run, for example. The act of reflecting on an issue outside its habitual context increases our capacities and the chance that we will hit upon the right solutions. But, at the same time, whilst doing this, it is essential to eliminate any distractions that could interfere with this creative and lateral thinking so that you can fully concentrate on the issue at hand.

Bear in mind that if you start thinking about important issues some time in advance, your subconscious will have more time to work on them, thus increasing the likelihood of finding better ideas or solutions. By letting go of the habit of only thinking about these issues at work, in the evening or a last-minute rush, you will boost the quality of your work.

"Either you run the day, or the day runs you."
JIM ROHN

In order to do this kind of exercise, I usually go to a café where I feel comfortable or make the most of a train or plane journey (many clients report that high-speed train journeys are the ideal setting for this exercise) or even early in the morning in a hotel after breakfast-As you can see, any setting that may be distinct from my office or my home environment. This is when I do a mind map, feel inspired to connect ideas, analyze issues and generally reach positive conclusions.

The law of 'stop and think': *Taking a step back to evaluate*

Stop and think involves stopping and mentally (and sometimes physically) taking a step back from our working routines and surroundings to analyze matters from a more objective standpoint. It is important to analyze ourselves and observe situations from the outside so that we can measure our progress or tweak our behaviour when we aren't moving in the right direction. But this is also about celebrating progress, remember that this will also have an impact on your motivation to keep going.

I have a number of ritualized *stop and think* moments:

- At the end of the day when I review what I've achieved over the course of the day, what I've completed and what I haven't managed to do as I fill in the daily review sheet with two or three lines that sum up the most noteworthy outcomes of the day. It shouldn't take more than five minutes, ten minutes at the most.
- At midday, to look at how the day is panning out. I usually spend two minutes.
- The weekly review to see how the week has gone and to plan the following week. This usually takes an hour. I like

to do this on Sunday evenings, and it is one of the habits that has most positively influenced my career.

- At the end of the month when I review what I have achieved from my table of "Objectives, MITs and *big rocks*" and I draft the plan for the next month, making any necessary amendments. This is probably one of the most important '*stop and think*' moments.
- When I go for a walk during moments of high stress, to clear my thoughts which helps me to see things from a fresh, calm perspective. As William Ury says: "Go to the balcony" to think when a negotiation is difficult.[19] I also do this when I sense that I am experiencing emotional hijacking and that I might act in an inappropriate way due to anger or frustration.

Other habits and rituals that help me

Some of my weekly rituals include:

- Exercising three or four times a week while listening to a podcast.
- Reading a minimum of three or four evenings a week.
- Meeting friends for lunch or dinner at least once a week.

In terms of daily rituals, these are the activities that are fixed into my schedule, no matter the day

19. Ury, W. (2007). *Getting Past No: Negotiating in Difficult Situations*. (New York: Bantam Books 1993).

- Drinking half a litre of cold water when I get up in the morning because we tend to become dehydrated overnight.
- Five minutes of stretches and sit-ups to get activated.
- Twenty minutes to write.
- Ten minutes to review the day.
- Two MIT session.
- Two UT sessions (with time slots for tasks grouped together such as returning calls, answering emails or checking my to-do list of less important issues).
- Ten minutes to review the day, plan the following day and makes some notes on the outcomes of the day.

The diary

All this personal and professional planning needs to be written down so that you can go back and consult it or update it. This is why it is essential to keep an actual diary as well as daily, weekly and monthly calendars. Many people ask me about apps and electronic programs to get organized instead of using a paper diary (which seems to be making a comeback). I will explain what I consider to be most useful in each case.

Traditional diary, or notepad

- This helps you to memorize because when you write something by hand you retain it more than if you had typed it up.

- It acts as a trigger because the diary itself is a visual reminder.
- It avoids 'online temptations', such as checking emails or WhatsApp.

Mobile apps

- Synchronizing a number of devices – your computer, tablet and phone – avoids having to input the same content across different platforms (although something as simple as having to write the same thing down in different places helps to keep all the issues you need to address top of mind).
- Setting appointments in your diary as reminders gives you a multitude of options in terms of time, space and various alerts, although this can lead to an over-dependence on our phones or computers.

Having said that, I must admit that both my clients and I have oscillated from one system to another at different stages. I am not entirely sure which is better and, although I'm currently using the FASE editable PDF agenda,[20] I also like the digital system and I am starting to use programs such as Slack, Teams and others that allow you to update project information or key MITs and share them with others

20. As I was developing the FASE method, I found that none of the agendas or diaries suited my needs. So I decided to create the FASE method agenda, available in two formats: paper or editable PDF.

(which has the added benefit of avoiding unnecessary emails, conversations and interruptions). While these programs facilitate collaborative work and communication, we shouldn't think of them as a solution to all our productivity problems. They are simply tools that can contribute to your own personal, which should be much more comprehensive. I would recommend trying a few of the many available tools and choosing the one that best suits your needs. To the teams I work with, I always emphasize the importance of using tools that have inbuilt reminders or enable them to share information as this will save them time. In addition, in order to be able to make the most of these tools, the whole team needs to be trained in using them and encourage to create a culture of use. Doing this is really worth the effort, as the effect on the team's productivity will be really significant.

The use of collaborative tools demands additional considerations. Once again, we need to observe ourselves and look into how we are using them as sometimes the alerts and notifications end up becoming distractions. These can lead us towards multitasking and may eat into our time for individual work with high concentration.

These tools can be highly valuable, but only if we spend time thinking about how to make the best use of them in a balanced and coherent way, with a series of shared and respected guidelines. Ultimately, we need to design strategies that help us to get the most out of these technologies without detracting from our productivity. Otherwise, we risk slipping silently and progressively into using them in a sub-optimal way, allowing multitasking and inefficiency to creep back in.

On the other hand, there are programs and apps that help us to take notes, such as Evernote, a program to file and record documents. Users usually highly praise this tool, especially for its features such as classifying and searching for any entry or item of interest, ranging from a copy of your ID documents to notes from an important meeting.

I often encounter people in meetings who prefer to take notes on their computers or apps to avoid having to transcribe them later. But what normally happens when people have their electronic devices to hand is that they easily slip into checking their emails or WhatsApps. I have to add that when you see someone take notes on a digital device, you tend to think that they aren't paying the necessary attention to the meeting. There is also as it has been proven time and again that nothing substitutes the power of thinking and reasoning that comes with using pen and paper, as demonstrated in the recent study "*The pen is mightier than the keyboard: Advantages of longhand over laptop note taking*", by Pam A. Mueller and Daniel M. Oppenheimer. Personally, I take the majority of my notes by hand, and I have even incorporated technology by using a tablet with a digital pen. This has been a great discovery with infinite possibilities, and in my view, it is the best notebook in existence. Either way, whether you use a paper notebook or a digital one, it is important to make a note of interesting ideas that come to you throughout the day because these ideas won't automatically pop into our heads when we go back home or the office.

Personally, I use a mind map as a springboard for all my ideas and I use a whiteboard at home which helps to structure these ideas in a very visual way. From there, I record them in my "Objectives and MITs" Excel spreadsheet and then I transfer them over to my agenda. I like to combine Outlook as a calendar with my FASE method paper diary and my iPad with a digital pen. This has substituted my paper notebooks and where I take notes, explore ideas, and sketch out multiple mind maps. The advantage of using Outlook, Calendar or other tools is being able to synchronize them with your phone, organize and review tasks easily and set up a system of alerts. The Outlook calendar also enables you to keep track of less important pending tasks that will become UTs through automatic alerts as the deadlines approach.

"Actually, highly successful people don't think about time much at all. Instead, they think about values, priorities, and consistent habits."

KEVIN KRUSE

Energy

"Energy, not time, is the fundamental currency
of high performance."
JIM LOHER

Energy, despite representing the last letter of the acronym which gives the FASE model its name, is the essential cornerstone in any process of improving productivity and that is why we need to learn how to manage our energy effectively.

It is very important that we manage three different types of energies: physical, emotional and cognitive. All three are interrelated and need to be in good shape if you want to be productive. Some people invest a great number of hours every day, but they are not, in fact, able to be productive because they have low energy. While others, thanks to their optimum energy levels, manage to do eight hours of work that is highly productive.

Energy is our driving force to develop our working capacity, so we need to accept that managing our energy is more important than managing our time, as Tony Schwartz and Catherine McCarthy rightly observe in their article *"Manage your time, not your energy"*.[21] Improving your energy levels, whether physical, emotional or cognitive, will have a direct impact your sense of vitality and stamina throughout your working day, as well your capacity for concentration and full attention and even how you tackle day-to-day problems. It is also important to pace yourself throughout the whole working day to maintain high performance all day and not to burn out after the first few hours. This is not only applicable to your working day, but also to certain projects where you need to have the energy to complete them.

Going back to the concept of our circadian rhythms, we need to determine the times of the day when our energy levels are at their peak and schedule the most important tasks for those moments or when you need to energize and enthuse your teams. Having stand-up meetings - morning meetings where you need to stand- with your team are a good way to kick off the day and plan the tasks ahead. As part of this self-analysis, it is also useful to identify which people or issues tend to deplete your energy so that you can either avoid them or at least troubleshoot them in advance-Examples of these include meetings with toxic colleagues or visits to challenging clients.

21. Schwartz, T., and McCarthy, C. (2007). "Manage your time, not your energy", Harvard Business Review, vol. 85, n.º 10, p.63.

It is important to have a good understanding of your team members so that you know which activities help each one of them to recover their energy when you can see that they are flagging. For some, this might be going to the gym during their lunch break, for others it might be calling a friend, having a coffee or a short walk between meetings or blocks of maximum concentration time. We also need to think about this on their remote working days and identify which activities help them recharge their batteries in this new working landscape. These circumstances, together with our personality, will determine the type of activities that will help us to feel recharged as we work from home. Some people I have encountered need to have some in-person social contact on the days they work from home and tend to avoid additional online contact. Seeking out weekend and holiday activities that reenergize you, both physically and emotionally, is vital. If we don't keep our energy topped up, it will be very difficult to achieve our maximum performance because we will simply run out of steam.

Three interrelated energies

As numerous studies show,[22] our physical, emotional and cognitive energies are interrelated, so we need to develop and strengthen them continuously, as all three affect each other in different ways. Everybody's energy changes and evolves over time depending on a variety of circumstances, such as the amount of travelling we are doing, worries we may have, and even physical problems caused by the change of season. For example some people feel their levels of energy can lower significantly in the winter.

Although emotional energy is key, it is also the hardest one to manage. The lack of physical or cognitive energy is easier to spot and can be worked through with physical and cognitive activities, i.e.doing physical exercise or reading a book. Emotional energy, on the other hand, is related to ourselves, our feelings and our relationships with others, personally and professionally. A positive home environment, stability in our relationship with our partner or spouse, a positive relationship with superiors at work, and a respectful and empathic relationship with colleagues are all crucial factors in cultivating the peace and emotional balance that helps our lives to run smoothly. When you start

22. I recommend the study "The Impact of physical activity and sport on health, cognition, socialization and academic performance: a theoretical revision" by W. Ramírez, S. Vinaccia and G. Ramón, published in 2004 in the *Revista de Estudios Sociales* (Journal of Social Studies) (n.º 18, pp. 67-75).

implementing the FASE method, one of the first tasks is to carry out an internal audit, reviewing the current state of these three types of energy, because this is the foundation upon which the other of the pillars of the method rest.

How to boost your physical energy

Our body is a vital professional tool. When our physical health fails, everything else is secondary. We need to take care of ourselves and maintain sufficient physical energy so that we can give the best of ourselves, both personally and professionally.

There are some guiding principles that you should follow:

- Rest: it's not only the hours you sleep – between seven and eight hours is recommended – but also the quality of your sleep which will ensure a restorative rest.
- Nutrition: a healthy and balanced diet, eating everything in moderation and avoiding anything in excess. For many people, eating five times a day, while avoiding heavy meals that force the body to expend lot of energy for digestion, is ideal. This will vary from person to person and what we need to do is find the formula that works best for us. It is also very important to drink plenty of water – the recommended amount is around two and a half liters a day – especially at work because staying well hydrated is essential to keep our grey matter functioning at its best. A good way to tell how important hydration is for example is looking at the hangover headache and the general

malaise we often feel after consuming alcohol is caused by dehydration.
- Taking physical exercise, either going to the gym or playing a sport you enjoy, at least three or four times a week.

Nutrition

Nutrition has a considerable effect on our optimum energy levels during the day. It is important to plan your meals ahead to help sustain energy levels throughout the day.

As I mentioned before, having five meals a day is what is recommended for most people. As well as a good breakfast, lunch and dinner, you should also have a mid-morning and mid-afternoon snack to avoid that slump in our performance, when it feels like our brains have run out of fuel. This does, however, depend on the individual. Over the past year, I have been practising intermittent fasting which has really boosted my energy levels. Fasting and the process of ketosis, as the recent research by *The New England Journal of Medicine* found, benefits our energy, cardiovascular and neurological systems as well as having an antiaging effect. It is also important to follow the recommended portion sizes; we have all felt sluggish after a heavy meal which can sap our concentration. It is better to eat less than more. I tend to avoid high-glycemic-index foods such as bread, pasta and rice, opting instead for lower-calorie vegetable and protein-based meals to avoid feeling tired and lethargic after a meal. A simple way to alleviate this feeling is to go for a short 15-minute walk after eating to aid digestion boost energy levels. Some of my business clients, who also happen to be very sporty, have great self-control and are stricter with their diet during the week but treat themselves at the weekend.

There are also a number of food supplements that can be very useful. From my own experience, as well as recommendations from professional nutritionists, I would suggest:

- Green tea and black tea: for their capacity to help keep you awake and alert, boosting concentration. Although the effect is slower to kick in than caffeine, it lasts longer and doesn't lead to a crash.
- Casein protein: this has been linked to improved performance in sport and an increased feeling of fullness, which can reduce post-workout hunger pangs.
- Multivitamins and magnesium: to boost your energy and ensure that you are getting the necessary nutrients.
- Omega 3: This is linked to improved cognitive abilities (memory and retention) and agility. It works best taken at nighttime.
- Melatonin: it helps you to sleep deeply when you need to. It is especially recommended to combat jetlag or at times when you are struggling to sleep.

I have always had chaotic eating habits. I was often an anxious and compulsive eater, and those close to me used to say: "You don't eat, you devour food and all the wrong foods at that." The phrase "we are what we eat" sparked my curiosity and I began to explore books on healthy eating and nutrition. Today, this is still one of the aspects of my life that I find harder to control, but with each step in the right direction, I can see positive changes. I have worked on this by observing myself, reading up on the topic, eating consciously and accepting help from friends who know how to look after themselves. This last example is a lesson in *walking among giants,* learning from people who eat a balanced diet and take care of their health can be highly beneficial.

My eating habits have changed in recent years as I have tried to find a daily nutrition plan to maintain my energy levels throughout the day. It was finally with intermittent fasting, which involves eating my meals within a set eight-hour window during the day and fasting for the remaining 16 hours,that I found the best way to keep my energy levels stable throughout the day. This is the method that has most enhanced my physical energy as well as my cognitive abilities. I now regret having spent so many years neglecting my diet because the improvements have been life-changing in terms of energy and physical appearance.

Exercise

We need to exercise not only to boost our average energy levels but also to stimulate the release of hormones such as serotonin, dopamine and endorphins. You should aim to exercise three or four times a week, a twenty-minute session is enough – so lack of time is not an excuse. You can start by walking at a brisk pace and gradually increasing the intensity. The changes in the physical and emotional states are incredible when I see my clients incorporate exercise into their routines,

I work on my energy from two standpoints. Firstly, I proactively take care of my physical wellbeing (exercise, diet and sleep) to ensure I have enough energy to meet the demands of the week's activities and the necessary concentration for my MIT sessions. Secondly, when I feel a drop in my energy during the day, I always seek out restorative activities such as going for a short walk, eating an energy bar, or calling a friend. Moreover, as many studies have demonstrated reparative physical activities can improve our cognitive abilities.

How to boost your emotional energy

This is probably the most complex and fascinating type of energy. We can and should work on it, but there is always an element of the unknown(some call it "luck" and others "providence") that plays a role in the important moments in our lives, both positively and negatively. The key is in having the courage to observe negative events from a more constructive viewpoint and being able to extract positive life lessons from them, however, hidden they may seem.

Emotional energy involves improving our emotional intelligence, self-knowledge, empathy, assertiveness, and self-motivation. People are increasingly educating themselves or working with professionals, such as coaches, to improve their emotional intelligence, which is always a positive move. A first step could be taking a course, attending a workshop to learn how to better manage emotional energy, or simply by reading books on the topic, such as Daniel Goleman's seminal work *Working with Emotional Intelligence.*[23] Growing in this ability to look into the various options available to you, is key for the future of our productivity.

"Minimize time with coworkers who negatively affect your mood. Make an intentional effort to devote as little as possible."
MICHELLE GIELAN

The first factor that needs to be considered with this type of energy is the ancient Greek aphorism: "know thyself". We need to be realistic and aware of our emotional state, a product of our relationship to our immediate environment. Our personal life has a great impact on our working life, and it can be the key to achieving harmony and stability, or, conversely, trigger a chaotic and dramatic situation that in the most extreme cases can lead to stress and anxiety-related illnesses. At the same time, there may be situations at work that trigger negative emotions in us and we need to make an effort to manage these in a positive way. You mustn't forget, also, that working long hours intensely can often mask a lack of method and productivity, which can lead to negative consequences for our emotional wellbeing, by depleting our physical energy and cognitive abilities.

23. Goleman, D. (1998) *Working with Emotional Intelligence.* Bantam books

> "To maintain a good level of energy during the day, look for pleasurable formulas (such as drinking tea or listening to music) to combine with moments of work."
>
> **SUSAN CAIN**

To address this, we need to boost our emotional energy and optimism, cultivating self-motivation as the essence of our lives. Don't forget that reparative activities, such as enjoying in a hobby or spending time with your children or friends, are essential to recover your sense of balance and start the next day with renewed emotional energy. There are lots of helpful techniques such as:

- Starting the day thinking about everything that is going well in your life and what you can feel content about.
- Imagining that the day will bring good news and enjoyable moments.
- Having a good sense of humour, as this will help to keep problems more manageable.
- Having control over your thoughts because they are directly linked to your emotional state.
- Seeking out the company of optimistic people who inspire you with their positive take on life.
- Using techniques such as visualization and anchoring.
- Using positive language and avoiding complaints and negativity.
- Taking microbreaks throughout the day that help you to

feel revived and alleviate the buildup of stress over the course of the day. They are like a quick recharge.

- When you go to bed, think of five positive things that have happened that day.

Good stress and bad stress

One of the world's leading stress experts Hans Selye,[24] identified two types of stress: *eustress,* "good stress", and *distress,* considered "bad stress" that impairs our cognitive abilities and leaves us feeling depleted.

Eustress is generated in the face of a new situation that is challenging for us and triggers the production of dopamine, serotonin, and adrenaline, hormones that, as Dr Alonso Puig[25] explains, give us a sense of vitality, drive, greater concentration, confidence and an uplifted mood. *Eustress* boosts our abilities and intelligence, but this release of feel-good hormones lasts an hour and a half at most, at which point we experience a comedown. This is when harmful cortisol is released, which has the opposite effect. This is why prolonged periods of chronic stress without effective management are highly detrimental, ultimately becoming *distress.* Conclusion: to stay balanced, every ninety minutes or so, engage in an activity that replenishes you.

24. Selye, H. (1964). *La tensión de la vida (el stress)*. Buenos Aires: Compañía General Fabril Editora

25. Alonso Puig, M., y Peñalver Martínez, O. (2005). "Gestionar el estrés: una necesidad y un reto", Training & Development Digest, n.º 51, pp. 16-17.

In my case, worries, fear of the future and the unknown, feelings of self-doubt about how I would handle new situations or simply the sheer exhaustion of having been so overloaded with issues to deal with meant that I was mainly experiencing *distress*. The surge of cortisol made me feel drained and more tired, I often lost my sense of perspective and became swamped in pessimism and limiting thoughts. In those moments, It was essential for me to take action to stop the inevitable mental collapse I was feeling. To improve my emotional and physical wellbeing, I started to do more exercise, spend more time with upbeat friends and use much more positive language. Now, I also try to incorporate simple reparative activities into my routine, such as going for a walk around the block, calling a good friend, listening to one of my favourite songs or eating an energy bar while I read the newspaper. This way, I offset the cortisol and feel able to return to the "good stress". Remember that unless we counteract the effects of cortisol with dopamine and serotonin, it will be difficult to overcome that mental block that may paralyze us.

Meditation

The practice of mediation is booming due to the multiple benefits for our mental health and emotional balance. I want to highlight what this actually means for any professional: meditation improves memory, attention, and emotional wellbeing, as well as reducing stress and anxiety.

In a *Psychology Today*[26] article, the psychologist Emma Seppälä highlights the scientifically proven benefits of meditation in five areas: health, happiness, social life, self-control and cognitive abilities. They are all directly related to many of the key elements of the FASE method, so I always recommend that my clients try this wonderful tool.

As well as meditation, I also found that practising yoga and having a massage helped me a lot at times of stress. And reading, of course, is highly beneficial because it is through silence that we encounter our true selves, this intimate "I" that we scarcely acknowledge in our daily routines.

Quality time for leisure and enjoyment

It is essential to incorporate hobbies and activities that bring you joy into your schedule because they will reinvigorate and rebalance you emotionally, helping you stay energized. Remember that these activities also stimulate the production of dopamine and serotonin which will automatically make you feel better.

An excessive workload and day-to-day problems can give rise to the false belief that we haven't got time for leisure activities such as going to the cinema, a museum or a concert, or simply meeting up with friends. This is a big mistake and a false economy because it is precisely these moments of leisure and rest that are vital in helping us to reset psychologically and oxygenate our thoughts.

26. Seppälä, E. M. (2013). "20 Scientific Reasons to Start Meditating Today", *Psychology Today*.

We all need to analyse which activities can help lower our stress levels in specific situations. It is easy to identify them because they are always linked to activities or people that we are naturally drawn to, that are fun and make us happy. In my case, there is nothing that makes me feel better than going on a trip with my two sons, away from the daily grind, and sharing an enriching experience together.

When we initiate a process of improving our personal productivity, it's important to establish what our personal goals are so that we can plan how to achieve them. If one of your goals is to spend time with your children and take them on trips away, you will need to plan this in advance and keep it top of mind so that nothing gets in the way of it. I recommend making a list of all your most enjoyable activities; it could be eating out with friends, going out for a bike ride on Saturdays, going shopping, or watching your favourite series. The activities that help boost your emotional wellbeing and recharge your batteries are essential when you have a demanding workload. Find the activities that bring you joy and make them part of your routine.

How to increase your cognitive energy

In order to tackle the challenges and decision-making processes of any job, we need to proactively work on our cognitive energy and abilities. Cultivating a habit of reading and an interest in learning new skills makes it easier for us to acquire knowledge and increase our cognitive abilities. This will have a positive impact on our work, in decision-making and even on our concentration in situations such as reading a complex report or keeping our attention focused in meetings where we need to express clear, informed opinions.

The basic premise- although it may sound strange to some- is the following: we need to "force" our mind to generate new learning and neural connections that will gradually improve our abilities. Practices such as daily reading, listening to podcasts, writing, participating in training seminars that demand intellectual effort will raise your cognitive threshold day by day, and any activity that requires attention or careful thought will come easier to you. Just as you need to exercise to stay physically fit, we also need to train our brains if we want to get the most out of them.

> "Cognitive energy is directly related to the level of blood glucose. Therefore, it is beneficial to have close healthy snacks to replenish your willpower and energy during the day."
>
> **JAY PAPASAN**

There is a range of positive habits that may boost your cognitive ability:

- Supplementing a balanced diet with Omega 3, Vitamins B6 and B12 or incorporating foods that contain these nutrients into your diet.

- Avoiding excess caffeine and sugar intake. They are a quick energy boost for your mind, but the inevitable crash will follow.
- Avoiding excess alcohol intake which, along with the negative impact on our physical and mental health, also impairs our cognitive abilities.
- Monitoring stress levels that can affect our memory and mental agility.
- Continuously seeking out new learning experiences: studying languages, new professional development opportunities, reading, taking up new hobbies or trying a new sport. Any new learning activity will boost our cognitive ability.

> "The act of taking notes by hand involves active listening, cognitive processing, and finally recalling it to record it. People who take notes with a laptop tend to just robotically record spoken words, without doing the mental work to process it."
>
> **KEVIN KRUSE**

Keep your anxiety in check

When you experience negative emotional states, your cognitive energy will drop, and as a result your ability to concentrate, even your memory will be impaired. Simple tasks will seem more complicated, and those that are truly complicated will feel impossible to deal with, leading you to put off tackling them day after day. It is like living in a state of perpetual emotional hijacking, causing your anxiety to spike, and over time this can feel like a normal way of leading your daily life. This kind of chronic anxiety is more common than we might think. The rational part of the brain is taken over by the emotional part of the brain and the psychological stress overwhelms us, leaving us unable to perform simple tasks that require basic order and planning.

When I was suffering anxiety due to my uncertain professional future, one of my wisest friends said: "Problems will get solved in the end, but you need to prioritize your mental health." I was so disorientated that I struggled to understand this at first, but thanks to this comment, I started to work on bringing my crippling anxiety under control. As I will explain in greater detail, I started to exercise every day, share my problems with friends and look for ways to lift my spirits and make myself feel better every day.

On one occasion, I met a prominent business leader who was at risk of going to prison for a possible tax offence. I asked him how he managed the distress and anxiety caused by the uncertainty of not knowing whether or not he would be imprisoned, and he told me, very clearly, that he forced himself to exercise and keep his brain occupied every day in order to stay busy and motivated. Ultimately, this was a way of avoiding emotional hijacking or fighting against it. And this is what I did: I went to spinning classes and worked on obtaining my doctorate. When I told my closest friends about the doctorate, they would look at me as if I needed to see a doctor, much less work on a doctorate. But I managed to do it. Now, my ability to concentrate and achieve full attention are at their peak, which shows that our brain is like a muscle that develops with practice.

> "Attention works much like a muscle, use it poorly and it can wither; work it well and it grows."
> **DANIEL GOLEMAN**

Keep an eye on your energy levels

Now that you understand the importance of keeping your energy levels balanced, you will need to carry out weekly internal "audits" so you can take action to raise your energy levels, if necessary, and maintain an awareness of how you are feeling at all times. Remember that an imbalance in any one of these three types of energy is a sure-fire way to diminish your effectiveness and productivity in the hours you spend working.

At those times of stress when you release cortisol and start to feel the harmful effect this has on your physical and emotional wellbeing, you should try to challenge and overcome limiting beliefs. We are all much more capable than we realize. During periods when we are suffering from low self-esteem or feeling sad, as incredible as this may seem, we can actually distort our perception of reality and even refuse to listen to or accept opinions or advice that may force us to face the uncomfortable reality of our state of mind. We are caught in a vicious circle, thinking that the only solution is to work harder while ruminating on our problems, which only serves to intensify our negative feelings. As in many cases, self-awareness, listening to the opinions and advice of others will be essential in helping you to overcome these difficult phases. When you come through these hard times, it will be important to learn how to take care of your mental and emotional well-being with the wisdom you have gained and the willpower you are developing.

When I was at my lowest point emotionally, I struggled to muster the energy to face a normal working day. I knew that I had to improve my physical wellbeing because it would make a positive difference in my emotional energy and by extension my cognitive abilities. I had to break out of the vicious circle of negativity and apathy and inhabit a virtuous circle of optimism and motivation. Exercising helped to boost my physical and emotional energy while working on my doctorate was a constant and intense challenge for my cognitive energy. When I started, my capacity for full attention was never more than 15 minutes, but I gradually made 1 % marginal gains, and sometimes I was even able to incorporate six HIT sessions into my day. This dramatically enhanced my abilities, increased my processing speed, improved my concentration under pressure and my memory, which also bolstered me emotionally. In short, the three types of energy fed into each other and gradually grew stronger and stronger.

> "Successfully working from home is a skill, just like programming, designing or writing. It takes time and commitment to developing that skill, and the traditional office culture doesn't give us any reason to do that."
>
> **ALEX TURNBULL**

We decided to revise the book in the latter part of 2020 because it is clearly a year that will go down in history as heralding a monumental shift in working practices. It is a period that has seen a rapid expansion of remote working, whether from home or other spaces, which would have seemed unimaginable before. At the start of 2020, many business leaders and professionals thought that working from home or managing teams remotely would be efar too complex. However, if you take a step back, you can actually see that areas such as those of commercial and international departments have been operating remotely for decades.

The sudden, dramatic rise in remote working from home – from 0 to 100-as the world entered lockdown took place, in many cases, under the worst possible circumstances: there had been no time to prepare, the whole family was now under one roof, or you and your partner were now forced to compete for internet bandwidth. And now, many companies are starting to choose the hybrid model a combination of remote and office working depending on a number of different factors from personality type, personal circumstances, the stage the company is at, or the particular role in the company and the tasks that need to be carried out.

Every day I meet more and more people who take it as a given that the old model of office working only, will never return. This is something that I can also relate to. It is clear now very clear to me that I will be travelling far less, transferring my work online, while delivering some conferences and workshops in person at certain times or when the circumstances demand it. I like to ask my clients and friends to reflect on the benefits that this flexibility is bringing. People are generally unanimous in citing the time that we are gaining back each month as we have drastically reduced commuting to work, moving between one meeting and the next and business trips. But there are still some that worry there may be some risks to this new way of working, to which I always respond that we now have have the best of both worlds by combining remote and office-based working effectively. It is important to remember that we can all gain from a model that remote working expert Alex Muench rightly notes, allows us to enjoy the freedom of being able to work from anywhere with the flexibility of being able to adapt our work to our personal lives and not the other way around.

In terms of effectiveness, this involves thinking more broadly about efficiency, not only in offices but in other locations where there may be other bad habits and distractions that we need to be aware of. It is also important to consider how working remotely effects our different energies, because having the flexibility to work from home can be really beneficial in some areas but have a negative impact on others. Since the pandemic, I have seen how people have made the most of this situation to improve their fitness, replacing their daily commute with a workout. While others working at home have struggled with feelings of loneliness that have led to a marked decline in their emotional energy and burnout in the medium term. Lastly, there are others who are making use of this greater flexibility to study or engage in programs of professional development. Again, knowing how to make the most out of this depends far more than we might think on the individual and less on the context. We need to maintain that internal locus of control I mentioned before.

4. In search of effectiveness in remote working

The sudden expansion of remote working March 11th 2020: my learning journey of remote working begins

On March 11th I was in Barcelona, like I have been, most weeks in recent years when clients started to cancel sessions, both on the actual day and the day after. I stayed in the hotel with nothing much to do, still unaware of what was coming, but trying to reserve a seat on the first train home. I started to hear talk of 'lockdown orders' in Spain, something that was already happening in other countries. I, honestly, didn't understand what this phrase meant at the time, but I started to think about what the future might look like, both for me and the companies I was working with. Would I be able to continue delivering training workshops, both in group and individual sessions? How would I be able to work from home without travelling? I could never have imagined that eight months later, I would have the same job but travelling only a quarter of what I did before, as well as many other surprises that came along the way; I managed to work with clients for four months straight, without ever meeting them in person, AND with very positive results. I gave a talk at a conference to five hundred people from my living room at home.

I have also found that the quality of my work has improved, which is linked to another aspect that has improved by 200 %: my physical and emotional energy. Not to mention that, with the time I saved in eliminating the daily commute, I wrote a book on resilience that was published in April 2021. And as I like to recommend doing in any new challenge, I spent time thinking about this new model of working. During the pandemic, we learned a lot about remote working. This learning has come from a variety of sources including mistakes or successes from personal experience, observing others and listening to what clients are reporting back in sessions. I have also researched case studies of companies that have successfully implemented a remote working model, such as the Finnish company Telenor, that are totally aligned with the principles in this book. But I think we have wasted an opportunity by not taking enough time to think properly about the clear advantages of applying this new hybrid model. I am positive that, in the future, this will be evident to all of us.

The aim of this chapter is to spark a series of reflections as well as offer ideas on how to achieve greater effectiveness in remote working. There are also some general considerations on the advantages and disadvantages of remote working.

Changing our beliefs

At the start of 2020, when nobody was thinking about Covid or the possibility of lockdown orders, some companies were reticent, for whatever reason, to allow employees to work from home for a few days every month. But this has now changed. **The unprecedented circumstances of the pandemic meant that remote working was introduced as a matter of urgency, and I believe that we will never return to a predominantly office-based working culture.**

If we look closely at the experience of those who have pioneered this practice in the past as mentioned before, the reality is that many employees have managed to maintain their productivity while working from home. However, many also acknowledged that it took longer than it should have to establish practical routines to work effectively on the days that they are based at home. In fact, I have to admit that I initially found it a challenge myself, to be disciplined and effective on the days that I decided to work from home. I would end the day with the sense that I hadn't fully harnessed the advantages inherent in working remotely: fewer interruptions, less time wasted moving from one location to another and greater opportunities for concentration.

From March 2020 to the present day, I have had the opportunity to speak with many executives and professionals on the issue of effectiveness while working remotely. What I was hearing sounded at first like a contradictory message but there is a certain logic to it. On one hand, during the first few months of the lockdown order, many executives highlighted that productivity in their teams was increasing, with the exception of those employees who had children or family situations that made it difficult to work from home.

Just as nobody expected the capacity and speed of organizations to adapt to this new way of working, it also came as a surprise that, in the face of not being able to leave home, the reaction of many people was to work non-stop, as if there were no other activities that they could have engaged in. Logically, this translated into better results, but this doesn't always mean greater effectiveness. For many people who struggled to disconnect from work, this also led to a silent and gradual deterioration in their wellbeing. The first important message is that at home, it is even more important to build these mini energizing activities into your day, as well as sticking to a clearly defined working schedule.

On the other hand, these same executives started to raise their concerns with me at the beginning of summer 2020 because their productivity levels were showing signs of decline. They had even noted a certain amount of apathy in their teams, despite many having gained back time and energy at not having to travel or move between meetings.

Based on my experience and these testimonies, it is clear

that after the period of confinement, many people had reached saturation point and, in some countries, where they had the option, decided to relocate to their holiday homes. And in this environment, there certainly were other activities besides simply working. Possibilities such as an afternoon dip in the pool with the children, and in one case I know of, a three-hour bike ride in the mornings, tested the willpower and motivation of some professionals. However, this is not necessarily a barrier to achieving objectives. I like to remind people that this is not about the hours you put in, it's a matter of effective work. Moreover, stories of people working twelve-hour days over sustained periods of time never tend to end well. **The key point to understand is that effective work and productivity are incompatible with chaotic working styles, disorganization and many of the bad habits that are part of human nature, as we have seen throughout this book.**

There are a number of essential prerequisites to working effectively: **the will to do it, being honest with yourself, and of course, effort and sustained action to change deeply ingrained habits.** Fortunately, many clients tell me that having a productivity method like the FASE method that they can share with their teams has been hugely helpful. The effort they have made has been more profitable than ever. Clients have said that without the FASE method, they would be far more uneasy with this new normal. Organizations will no longer decide unilaterally which working model to implement definitively: whether this is 100 % office-based working, 100 % remote working or a combination of the two. At the time of writing, this continues to be an evolving situation and working practices will no doubt be guided by the measures introduced by governments around the world.

However, the uncertainty is not what I find most worrying. **I think we need to be more concerned about working proactively, both on an individual and organizational level, to improve our productivity and think carefully about how to adapt our working practices to any fit setting or circumstances that arise.** The stoics had the right idea when they said that we should focus exclusively on what is within our control and influence and forget the rest, but I'll leave this topic for my new book on resilience.

In short, Let's not spend too much time on the whys and wherefores of the pandemic, other events of global magnitude or individual circumstances that may arise. Excessive ruminating rarely solves anything. **Let's, instead, focus on incorporating a method that helps us to align our priorities, helps us learn to prioritize individually, regain the ability to work with full attention, know how to say no assertively and, above all, balance our personal lives with our professional lives with a sense of control, without stress or guilt.**

And this is why, the issue should not be whether working from home can be as effective as working from the office, **the crux of the matter is the need to develop good practices, tips and ideas that can help us to be more effective from the very first day of remote working. Otherwise,** without a coherent method, you risk succumbing to pitfalls that can diminish your effectiveness and productivity, setting yourself up for problems in the medium term.

Irrespective of the pandemic, I have been working with a few clients who had decided to work at least one day a week from home. There were many reasons for this, including a lack of space at the office, achieving a better work-life balance, saving time by eliminating the daily commute and implementing new working policies on an organizational level. It has been a process of trial by error and learning from the example of countries and organizations that have a strongly embedded culture of remote working.

Key points to consider when working from home

These are the main conclusions of the learning and discussions with many clients and friends over the last two years. We have distilled this into ten tips or points to consider that everyone should be able to apply to their personal situation. Evaluating ourselves is the first step towards effective change.

1. **Set up a designated workspace in your home**, taking ergonomic factors and online access into account. If it is a place where you feel at ease, better still, as this will promote a sense of calm and concentration. Try to have some specific routines to denote work; for example, dressing as if you are going to the office can have more of an influence than you think. If you could possibly find a work-only space, even better. This way it will be

easier to differentiate it from the rest of your personal surroundings. Think about any previous routines you had systematized that will now be different in this new setting, such as where you go to eat, the coffee machine or having office supplies, if this applies to you.

2. **Create a schedule for yourself as if you were working office hours, with start and end times, breaks and a lunch hour.** it is essential to have clearly defined boundaries to maintain a balance between your working hours and your personal life. Otherwise, you may find that if you mix the two, you won't manage to be effective at work or enjoy your personal time with family. Make sure that those you work most closely with know your hours. As well as avoiding misunderstandings, you will also see colleagues make an effort made to respect them Managing expectations is key.
3. **Consider any possible distractions that might affect you and come up with solutions.** While some office distractions have now disappeared, other distractions at home will soon replace them, such as spending more time on household chores, personal relationships, or hobbies that you have always longed to try. Bear in mind that this new work setting offers temptations that were not within reach before. Make a list of them and think about how you can minimize their risk of distraction. Being aware of and avoiding temptation is a great place to start. Distractions can include anything from your own pet to the people that you share your space with during working

hours but whom you didn't see during the day before, as well as the many personal temptations you didn't have before. Including binge-watching a Netflix series. Netflix can be the worst of temptations.

4. **Agree on specific times to meet and consult with the people you work most closely with, as well as some ground rules around availability.** Bear in mind that, when you are not physically in the same place, the old forms of interaction no longer apply and you will need to create new and aligned ways of interacting remotely to avoid disruptive interruptions.
5. **Invest time in honing remote teamwork and collaboration.** Take time, regularly, to consider what is working well and what could be improved for the next meeting or collaborative project.
6. **Gain awareness by reflecting daily on how you are managing this new way of working so that you can draw practical conclusions and make improvements.** Use Fridays as an opportunity to reflect back on the events of the week and set the goals for the following week with the aim of being more effective, implementing any necessary changes such as a new schedule, a different location or reducing distractions.
7. **Pay attention to any changes in your emotional wellbeing.** It is important to avoid a deterioration in your mood due to the isolation of working alone, possible stress brought on by the change or the uncertainty of whether you will be able to achieve your results in this

new model of working. But we can also look at it from a different point of view, and see the positive aspects and emotional advantages to be gained from spending more time at home. Activities that were previously off-limits are now within reach. You should strengthen these. For me, having the chance to have dinner with my children during the week or being able to meet friends for lunch are some of my greatest catalysts in terms of improving my emotional energy. The career development expert Carlotta Zimmerman cautions that working at home can give rise to feelings of loneliness and underlines the need to develop a plan to create a positive and inviting working environment to promote a sense of emotional balance.

8. **Keep a positive attitude, because there will certainly be some professional growth during these unprecedented times that take us out of our comfort zone.** Ironically, our home, in this case, is not a comfort zone when it comes to working. But at the same time, there are clear advantages to working from home, depending on our individual circumstances and how we face challenges. For many of us, the future will bring a combination of working from the office and working from home, offering the best of both worlds.
9. **Recharge your physical and emotional energy often.** You will need to build some physical activity into your day, micro-exercises such as going up and down the stairs are ideal. Leisure activities such as calling friends or family, listening to music, or relaxing with a coffee while leaving

technology to one side so that you can fully rest are just a few examples. When you plan these microbreaks to recharge your batteries, they no longer feel like wasted time and instead become an effective way to stay productive for the rest of the day. These replenishing activities are far more feasible while working from home. Identify ways that you can take a break, try them out and see what effect they have on you. What certainly won't help are marathon working days spent glued to our computers, only getting up to visit the bathroom. There are many more opportunities to build exercise into your day because as well as gaining time, we also have many more exercise options to keep fit at home. I know many people who have managed to improve their physical, as well as mental, well-being while working remotely.

10. **When contacting colleagues or associates, take advantage of video conference apps to make the interactions feel as real as possible,** using Skype, Zoom or similar programs that offer visual contact. Remote working has become a reality for many companies due to the extraordinary circumstances arising from the pandemic. It is clear that this will lead to new working practices that are here to stay so everything you can do now to optimize how you work will stand you in good stead for the future.

However, we need to bear in mind that this technology also has the potential to become yet another digital distraction, along with email and Whatsapp, during our working day.

There is a risk of becoming swamped with continuous video calls and, in some cases, excessive interaction. This "digital overload" can also exacerbate a lack of attention and concentration on the really crucial issues.

Many readers will also be thinking of other ideas that they have been putting into practice to improve their productivity, trying them out to see the result. A client told me recently that she had decided not only to get a different personal phone but also a personal computer so that when she sits down to watch Netflix in her personal time, her working life isn't just a click away. Another client had enough space at home to set up a workspace, meaning that all his work was confined to this space. Another useful tip is to create a ritual that signifies the end of your working day and the return of your personal time. What works for me is reflecting on how the day has gone based on what I had planned. I then prepare for the following day and use the act of closing my laptop as a sign that "my working day has finished". After this, I go straight to my bedroom and change into my sports clothes, which is also the trigger that underlines the need to exercise daily even if it's only for ten minutes (which always ends up being more).

As Carol Dweck, pioneer of the "growth mindset versus fixed mindset", would say, we need to face unexpected changes with a constructive attitude and the knowledge that it is precisely in these moments of difficulty and change that real personal growth and progress occurs. And if this growth is shared with our colleagues, the progress can be exponential.

Among my clients, I am noticing the emergence of two, polarised groups. The first group is working excessively under this new hybrid model. They are investing more hours than necessary, and they are finding it hard to switch off. I always remind them that effectiveness and improving the way we work demands that we disconnect from time to time, otherwise sooner or later our emotional wellbeing will pay the price, which means our effectiveness will take a hit.

The other group is moving in the opposite direction. Without them realising, their personal lives have bled into their working hours and this has affected their performance. I always remind them that it is more important to control their environment than their willpower, so it's essential to get to the bottom of what is distracting them in their home or personal environment.

A final thought on remote working

On many occasions, both in recent years and before the pandemic, I have experienced first-hand the pros and cons of remote working. On the positive side, it is a way that offers the opportunity to get the most effectiveness out of people if combined well with working from the office. The downside is that our very human nature can lead us unconsciously towards a silent and progressive deterioration in our way of working remotely, with very negative results. Also, from a more individual point of view,I have also noticed that there are factors that have a significant influence on our ability how we make the most of the many positive benefits of remote working. Some of these factors are a result of our own nature as people, whilst others arise from our environmental circumstances or a particular point in time. Our personality, the environment and circumstances at home, the time it takes to get organised, even the nature of our work and the habit of travelling distance between our home and the office are all important factors to bear in mind.

Aside from those who had to work from home during lockdown while trying to care for small children at the same time, it might be difficult for some of us to appreciate these potential pitfalls. Many people working remotely have put in longer hours than ever because of lockdown guidelines, which stopped them from doing anything else from Monday to Sunday. But in a post-Covid world there will be many activities competing with our work and, if we don't remain vigilant, a gradual and imperceptible drop in our productivity can occur. Moreover, the attitude of maximum cooperation and camaraderie will also fade. Not everything will be so idyllic in this sense.

Other people, as they read this new chapter, will be able to understand the risk that we face with this new, apparently more independent way of working. But, as with almost everything else, it is only a matter of time before things adjust and we are able to make the most out of a hybrid working model in the future. It is important to take responsibility for our productivity, both in the office and remotely and be prepared to take action before we start losing or maximum efficiency,

And this is precisely what I consider the riskiest side of hybrid working as it doesn't reflect the experience and learning from what has been described as the greatest experiment of remote working. By contrast, organizations and their leaders need to encourage three simple actions at this point in time as we carefully begin to return to normality.

1. **Think about what your ideal combination of remote and office-based working would be.** If we really want to optimise the effectiveness of either option, there may two points to consider. Firstly, address any potential conditioning factors that may influence how you do your job remotely, something that doesn't tend to present any difficulties, as the pandemic has demonstrated in the majority of cases. Secondly, consider what the optimum combination would be according to each individual's personality and their circumstances to boost their effectiveness and engagement. For example, if someone saves two hours a day in commuting time, it seems reasonable to assume that being able to work from home a few days a week would improve their physical and emotional energy.
2. **New ways of communicating.** In many cases, the period of individual confinement also has created greater and better contact and internal communication within teams. How has this been possible? Technology has helped

considerably, but we have also stepped up as colleagues and leaders. We have paid greater attention to our teams, which links back to a greater willingness to cooperate. And here we are invited to reflect, in a measured way, with a pen and paper (or maybe a tablet and digital pen), on all of this to see what we can learn and modify our past working models in areas where it may have been lacking.

3. **Discovering and adapting the new working model is a project in itself.** As we move forward, deciding on a new working model needs to be approached as a project in itself that requires regular reassessment, both individually and as a group. It will be a case of trial and error to develop a new definitive working model, taking issues into consideration at both an individual and group level. This may seem paradoxical, but we need to stop and think so that we can save time later. Maybe we are attending too many webinars, or trying to be there for each other in whichever way possible, and we need to spend more time defining our new working strategy. It is important to make use of tried and tested strategies, such as those in this book, to carry out a self-evaluation and consider improvements.

Perhaps the greatest lesson in all this is that, at last, we have managed to challenge the over-use of office-based working. The goal now is to develop dynamic and consistent reporting structures, align objectives, assess progress, and guide and support these improvements. This way we will understand that spending a fixed number of compulsory hours in the office makes no sense. Because we all now know that what really matters, whether we are confined to our homes during a pandemic or not, is true effectiveness and perseverance that can also result in a working arrangement that we all want and deserve.

5. Starting and implementing the FASE method

"The path to success is to take massive, determined action."
TONY ROBBINS

Gain time in your day and boost your energy

Firstly, to implement the FASE method, you need to fully comprehend your current situation and have the motivation to create a positive change. Then, through a series of exercises, you will be able to incorporate a number of key habits and rituals that will gradually drive you towards success.

This process usually lasts two months. Being truly motivated, making use of helpful tools (such as the FASE diary and Scheduling apps) and appropriate monitoring means success is guaranteed. If you try to implement a process of change of this magnitude too quickly, within a week, for example, you will more than likely fail because our minds are not designed to assimilate such drastic changes in a short space of time. Remember that this process involves unlearning and eliminating a series of deeply ingrained habits before incorporating new ones.

FIRST EXERCISE

Objective: gaining time in your day and boosting your energy

Develop an action plan to improve your energy levels

The first thing you need to do is some self-observation to identify any areas for improvement. You will need to measure and score your levels in each one of the three types of energies that we have previously mentioned: physical, cognitive and emotional.

To be able to work a full day at peak performance without experiencing a slump after the sixth hour (as is often the case), you will need high energy levels. Remember that, when you have enough energy, your ability to concentrate will improve and won't be affected by tiredness or difficulty in maintaining your full attention while you carry out your most important tasks.

Each day is like an eight-hour race in which you have to keep up a good pace at every stage of the course – in the office, in meetings, during lunch. In order to do so, not only do you need to maintain the necessary physical energy but also to be able to manage your emotional energy, despite the challenges that may arise over the course of the day or those that emerge at specifically difficult times of the year. At the same time, if your cognitive energy is dipping, your ability to concentrate or carry out certain mental activities, such as reading a report or contract or following a long presentation, will be impaired as the day wears on. Remember that these different types of energy are all interrelated, so it is important to keep all three balanced.

Action plan:

- Improve your diet and make sure you stay hydrated.
- Do physical exercise.
- Sleep well.
- Read for at least 15 minutes before you go to sleep.
- Tackle and solve emotional problems by reflecting on them at least once a week.

How to correct bad habits and eliminate distractions

Once you have drafted your action plan to improve your energy levels, observe yourself over the course of a week and record all the non-added value tasks that you are carrying out so that you can get a clear idea of your main bad habits and distractions. To identify these tasks, I would recommend drawing up a mind map of all the tasks that you are currently undertaking. Then, highlight those that you could delegate or less important tasks that could be carried out at times when your energy is not at its peak. Remember that any circumstance that eats into your time and diverts you away from your objectives, should be considered a distraction.

This simple analysis is key to gaining back time. Notably, the benefits of delegating are two-fold, both freeing up the person who is delegating and offering responsibility and motivation to the person who is picking up the task. If you don't have a team to delegate to, try to spend a minimal amount of time on these less critical tasks during the moments when you have less capacity.

It is important to set aside time, at least once a week, to look closely at your bad habits and distractions as it can be very easy to slip back into repeating past mistakes. You will need to change these habits and be aware of any changing circumstances that may give rise to new bad habits. Eradicating bad habits is no simple task (especially when it comes to distractions) because most of them are so deeply ingrained that it can be difficult to eliminate them fully. Achieving this requires daily awareness and effort but it is indeed doable if you truly embrace the process enthusiastically. The Initial doubts and niggles on how difficult it may be to tackle the issues will disappear as you start to make headway. I would also recommend asking those around you for help- you would be surprised at the response and the results you will get. When you ask colleagues for their mutual cooperation to avoid distracting each other, there is often great understanding and collaboration despite the initial reticence we might feel about discussing these issues. It is the same with people with whom we may share a space during remote working hours.

To pinpoint which distractions and bad habits are a problem for you, I recommend using a notebook or making notes on your phone, to record these types of behaviour every time you become aware of them. On Friday, at the end of every week, copy your notes over to a double-entry spreadsheet and add an action plan of how you are going to eliminate each bad habit. If you skip this step, you will never be able to achieve eight hours of effective work each day and by extension, reach the objectives you have set yourself.

There are five or six distractions and bad habits that are particularly common among most professionals. Over time, I have seen that the solution to eradicate them almost always involves taking drastic measures. Here are the main culprits:

Email

If you don't want your job to turn into a constant cycle of reading and answering emails, while occasionally working, you'll need to set some ground rules. Checking your inbox constantly to avoid a build-up of unread emails is not the best way to go about this, neither is investing too much time in creating perfectly organised email folders instead of using this time for your 80/20 tasks (you can reread chapter three on the Pareto Principle if it helps).

One rule could be checking your email three times a day,

or every hour, instead of doing it compulsively every five minutes. Moreover, it is important to let your superiors and clients know that you won't be able to answer emails straight away, especially if they are used to getting an immediate response from you. Nobody will most likely object to this. I would also recommend removing the new email notifications because they are distracting and lead to multitasking. To those who struggle to resist the temptation to check emails, I always recommend switching off the internet and reconnecting every hour to see if there is anything urgent to deal with. Nevertheless, I can't emphasise enough the need to stop being so dependent on your inbox.

WhatsApp

I know it's not an easy feat but you will need to switch off your personal WhatsApp notifications during working hours. If you have your professional WhatsApp account on your work phone, you can check it every hour or ask people to call you if an important or urgent matter arises.

The most effective option is to remove the alerts and notifications, even the unread messages badge (you can do this with all the WhatsApp groups where you receive excessive messages, or simply leave these groups). Check it only every hour and for a maximum of ten minutes.

At times of maximum concentration, the best thing is to put your phone in aeroplane mode and keep it in a drawer or away from you to avoid the temptation of looking at the screen.

Social media

It will never cease to amaze me how much time we waste on social media or the number of times we tend to check our social media updates. LinkedIn is clearly relevant for some positions but logging in to check a particular detail can often turn into half an hour of mindless scrolling. Facebook is continually developing techniques to make images more attractive and videos to play automatically, grabbing our attention and causing us to waste valuable time that should be spent on our most important tasks. Do not forget that the creators and developers of these platforms are literally working to get us hooked. You will need to put some strict rules in place and keep to them.

A very useful way to keep our focus on work and make our time on social media more pleasurable is to try to log in during your lunch break and after work, before dinner. The rest of the day should be free from all social media. In recent years, I have come across many clients, over the years, who were unaware of how much time they were wasting during working hours, on Instagram, Facebook, Twitter and even Tinder. The 2020 Netflix documentary *The Social Dilemma* looked at the dangerous impact of social media and exposed the addiction that many of these platforms induce as opposed to their value as useful tools.

Managers or colleagues

There will always be a manager or a colleague who, when an idea pops into their head, will want to interrupt you, without asking or thinking that you might be working on something important you need to concentrate on. Or maybe you are the one who interrupts others when you don't know what to do or you feel bored or tired.

Because it may be easier or even more pleasant to speak to others rather than do concentrated work on something important- it is after all human nature-,I would encourage you to gently approach the interrupters in your life and ask them to group their queries together so that they can check in with you either in the morning or the afternoon, but only once a day. This tends to have a very positive effect and from that moment onwards; the interrupter will think carefully before approaching you and there will be fewer interruptions. On the other hand, with the expansion of remote working, the number of unexpected interruptions has decreased, while the number of video calls has gone up when, in many circumstances, the issue could often be solved more quickly by phone.

Meetings

Meetings can often be too long or ineffective, even unnecessary at times, and we often complain because they never seem to achieve the necessary results. I have spent years analyzing the dynamics of meetings and asking professionals to get to the bottom of what it is they find irritating about meetings. The majority of replies have centred on the battle of egos, the lack of structure in the discussion, the failure to reach definitive conclusions, the lack of a moderator and seeing participants send emails and WhatsApp messages instead of paying attention to the meeting. And finally, because of the usual poor planning, meetings tend to be excessively long, and people end up zoning out.

Another reason why meetings can be unproductive is that managers might be highly skilled at their jobs, but they may have no framework to prepare for and chair meetings. The biggest mistake they tend to make is to see meetings as something so basic and secondary, that they don't bother to prepare properly for them. In conclusion, here are a few tips to improve your internal meetings and boost their effectiveness:

- In the email meeting request, make the objectives clear and state the approximate length of the meeting.
- At the start of the meeting, recap the aims and briefly explain why each participant has been invited.
- Nominate a moderator to monitor speaking times and intervene to stop attendees from exceeding their allocated slot so that everyone has a turn to express their point of view (which also avoids post-meeting comments) and tactfully redirect the focus of the meeting if it goes off track.
- Keep electronic devices off unless they are absolutely essential for the meeting.
- Set the duration of the meeting in advance. It is useful to have a clock visible to ensure participants keep to the allocated time and the agreed topics.
- Draw conclusions from the meeting and record them on

a whiteboard visible to all, after which the moderator or minutes taker should send them to all participants via email along with the agreed action points, deadlines and those responsible for each task.

In our current new way of working, It is also important to think carefully about the increasingly frequent online video meetings. Firstly, all the previously mentioned strategies will, of course, need to be adapted to online meetings. It will be helpful to spend time considering specific improvements, such as the following:

- Have each participant introduce themselves at the beginning.
- Keep the camera on.
- More than ever, avoid multitasking and checking email as there will be increased opportunities and temptations.
- Encourage the participation of all those present.

With effective management, we can progress from meetings that are often a financially wasteful practice (given that they often involve many people mired in multiple discussions for hours with no tangible results) to enjoying effective meetings that yield positive results.

Ourselves

It's really, really hard for most people to become actively aware of what we are doing. Above all, we find it hard to sustain our attention on a single activity, so we need to gradually train our ability to concentrate. This is the rationale behind the 45-minute HIT sessions of full attention.

As it can be difficult to admit to ourselves how much time we waste on social media, checking emails, or scrolling on our phone, I would encourage you to install an app such as Checky or RescueTime to measure and monitor your use (and 'abuse') of social media. When you start to see the results, it will probably become easier for you to react and reassess how you actually need to put your phone to one side while you are working.

By carrying out these initial exercises and really keeping your bad habits and distractions in check, you will make a major breakthrough in terms of gaining time back each day without having to work extra hours. You can regain up to 25 % of your time back, which translates into two or two-and-a-half hours a day. It is a very effective strategy but difficult to put into action because we actually believe that we are in control of the situation but the truth is that new technologies have been shown to be as addictive as narcotic substances. And so, on a final note, I would advise you to conduct a monthly review of how you are dealing with the new corrective measures, because, at times, we might fall back into bad habits. Some people have even created a weekly checklist to monitor their progress and commit to keeping their efforts up.

Personally, I like to complete a checklist on bad habits and distractions in my FASE agenda every day, as well as spending 15 minutes every Friday carrying out a weekly review. Self-observation has been key for me, as I often catch myself falling back into bad habits.

If you want to go further and make definitive changes, I would also recommend analyzing the correlation between the ways in which you tend to waste time and your emotional state in those moments. It is often our emotional state that is the true cause of our tendency to waste time.

SECOND EXERCISE

Objective: Dedicate quality time to what really matters

After you have managed to gain back two hours a day of quality time thanks to your increased energy levels, you should now focus on boosting your efficiency by spending your available time on what really matters.

Setting objectives: MITs and big rocks
What to focus on

An *objective* is something that you are expected to achieve as part of your role or a personal or professional goal that you would like to achieve. For example, for a sales director, their objective might be to reach the agreed sales targets or to have a highly motivated sales team.

In this second exercise, which usually takes place two weeks after starting the process, you will need to do something that may seem too obvious, but that many experienced people have never done: make a list of priority objectives within your areas of responsibility and the Most Important Tasks

(MIT) necessary to achieve these objectives. Some of these objectives are projects in themselves, and as such the tasks in many cases will be sequential. And once you carry out the task, it will disappear from your list. By contrast, other objectives will be ongoing and inherent in your role, so your tasks will always be something to factor into your weekly plan.

> "It's not about working harder. It's about working harder on how to work smarter."
> **SCOTT MARKER**

Sometimes I encounter people who find this exercise hard or who confuse objectives with tasks, and vice versa. I always advise them not to get too caught up in the classification, but at the same time avoid falling into the trap of "anything goes".

By doing this exercise and agreeing upon a strategy with others, you will have a table of "MITs and Objectives" that best reflects your reality. The simple act of creating the spreadsheet will provide useful information in terms of how you should distribute your time. Remember that these MITs should be the main focus of your work. Moreover, I also recommend listing them in priority order in the spreadsheet with the most important objectives at the top and the key tasks on the left. This way you should have your *big rocks*, the most relevant objectives, in the top left.

A month after implementing the suggested exercises (a certain amount of time is needed to complete them and improve them), you will find that you have more time to be productive and the necessary energy to work with full attention and motivation during the day. You will also have identified your main objectives and listed them in order of priority, as well as the tasks to achieve them. Ultimately, you will have gained quality time and you will be very clear on what you need to be dedicating yourself it to.

But be careful you don't fall into this trap: some people are able to achieve good results despite being continually distracted or in multitasking mode. I often asked myself how they were able to do it and the response is always the same: they are either working too many hours each week (something that is unsustainable in the long-term and always causes problems) or their years of experience and high level of intelligence enable them to work in this way. But they will never achieve their maximum potential and will always experience problems as a result of their chaotic approach.

THIRD EXERCISE

Objective: incorporate new habits into our planning

You will now have become efficient in your use and distribution of time, and you know where you need to focus in terms of the really important tasks. Now it is time to create daily, weekly and monthly rituals so that this new way of working becomes completely embedded in your habits and sustainable over time. The first task will be to identify the key moments of each day, week and month and transfer them over into your calendar. These time slots need to be sacred in your schedule and need to be adhered to.

All truly productive people have a series of habits that have become systematized, enabling them to work in a natural and integrated way according to the principles of productivity: focusing on what really matters, with full attention during the key times of the day and with optimum energy levels. These habits, each with their own recurring frequency, need to be included in your diary and calendar[27] the same as any

27. The FASE agenda structure is designed to remind you about these habits and rituals.

other activity and you need to be strict about keeping to them as they represent the foundation of the whole method:

- **Monthly:** Review and set monthly objectives and MITs, highlighting the *big rocks* of the month. I recommend doing this on the last Friday of every month, to review the previous month and plan the next month according to your observations. I call this the 'monthly stop & think'.
- **Weekly:** set the weekly plan by reviewing the MITs and the UTs that you need to tackle the following week, such as your schedule of meetings and one-to-ones with key people. I would recommend doing this on a Friday afternoon or on a Sunday.
- **Daily:** draft a daily plan highlighting the MITs and UTs that you will tackle, as well as the list of calls to make and emails to send. It is best to do this at the end of every day to start the following day with a clear plan.
- **Daily MIT sessions:** set your morning and afternoon blocks of time where you will incorporate your 45-minute MIT sessions. I would recommend clearing your calendar and avoiding taking on other tasks as much as possible during these time periods.
- **Create habits:** Turning these rituals into habits will help you to stick to this method until it becomes your natural way of working.

"Motivation is what gets you started. Habit is what keeps you going."

JIM ROHN

If we know what we need to do, why don't we do it?

At the start of my journey to achieve maximum productivity, I was surprised at how often I procrastinated and postponed completing certain very important tasks, despite knowing full well what I had to do each day and each week to make significant progress. The explanation can be found in chapter three on the difference between the executive brain – the frontal lobe –, and the emotional brain – the limbic system. As the most important tasks tend to be more complex, boring or frustrating, our emotional brain avoids tackling them and prefers to take on easier or more pleasant tasks. Pleasure versus tedium is a clash between these two parts of the brain. And the emotional part tends to win most frequently.

This is why many of my clients who, just like me, understand perfectly what they need to do, having created brilliant plans, let the days pass by going on autopilot, working long hours on what they feel like doing or whatever comes their way, and not on what they should be doing. But there are many ways[28] to help the executive brain triumph over the emotional brain, ranging from the most radical strategies such as taking into account that, if you don't take action, you will have to face very negative consequences if

28. I highly recommend the productivity book by Chris Bailey, *The Productivity Project*, published by Random House (New York) in 2016.

you don't change, to making small daily commitments by spending 20 minutes on an important task.

A daily attitude of continuous improvement

If you want to be really productive, you have to work on it every day, because frequency and perseverance are what will enable you to make greater strides. However much you hope to do well in an exam, deliver a project to your manager or pass a test, if you haven't worked day by day on cultivating perseverance and developing positive routines in your planning, both personally and professionally, you will come up against problems or find things more difficult. It is essential to get into the habit of delivering on your obligations, and the FASE method and the FASE scheduling process are two useful tools at your disposal. In a simple, practical and effective way, you will be able to go from a lack of motivation and having goals that seem unachievable to a well-ordered life with a time and place for everything. You will be able to enjoy leisure and hobbies that you thoroughly enjoy, guilt-free in the knowledge that you have done what you need to do.

Epilogue

Today I look back on that period of crisis as a fortunate time in my life, not because of what happened to me, but because of my ability to try and make sense of the challenges I was facing and find solutions. In addition, this enabled me to create a system of working that has helped many people to improve their quality of life in a remarkable way and boosted their personal and professional growth without having to have gone through the complicated situation I experienced. I am now a much more complete person,than I was before that crisis. I feel truly satisfied with my life and more able to enjoy every minute of it.

I want to offer you a few final thoughts on what was key for me, in my process with dealing with a crisis and might be helpful for you:

- Letting people in and showing my vulnerability to those around me.
- Setting clear objectives and action plans and reviewing them regularly.

- Being systematic and productive in putting these plans into practice.
- Writing everything down, both digitally and on paper.
- Seeking out the right people and distancing myself from toxic people.
- Committing to not over complaining and staying positive.
- Reflecting on what had gone wrong and accepting my part of the responsibility.
- Accepting my new situation with humility.
- Improving in areas that I considered of key importance
- Stepping outside my comfort zone, taking risks, and forcing myself to change.
- Showing kindness to others and trying to help them despite the difficult situation I was in.
- Keeping the concept of the internal locus of control firmly in mind.

If I had the ability to transform my life, you do too. I would strongly encourage you to give it a go because this whole process has enabled me to:

- Increase my resilience in face of serious obstacles
- Let go of countless fears.
- Cope much better with difficult situations.
- Be humbler and more honest with myself.
- Reflect more about things
- Grow in the face of difficulty.

- Express a zest for life and enjoyment.

So don't let any doubts hold you back and don't forget, it all depends on us-With willpower, a positive attitude and hard work, we can achieve any goals we set for ourselves.

Organization and planning are fundamental, and the FASE method became my best ally. I am sharing it with you because I am happy, and I want you to be happy too. Life is amazing, especially when you are able to reach your full potential, both personally and professionally. Don't let fears or passivity stand in the way of your chance to triumph in life and be a successful person.

I hope the journey that we have taken together marks a step-change in your productivity and your capacity to achieve happiness and satisfaction in your work. Every day I manage to learn and absorb new ideas and advice from my own clients, so I encourage you to send me your comments, questions or observations, and I will respond to them personally. I greatly appreciate the time you have taken to read this book because I truly understand how valuable time is.

"Time is the scarcest resource; and unless it is managed, nothing else can be managed."
PETER DRUCKER

Acknowledgements

Finally, I would like to say that 2020 also brought me some joy. One of the greatest surprises of the year happened on July 23rd when a friend called to tell me that *Lead Yourself* was the number one bestselling book in Amazon Spain in the professional development category. But the biggest surprise of all is having written a book that is now in its seventh edition. This is all the more meaningful because writing never came easily to me. I actually started writing articles with the aim of improving my writing. As James Clear rightly says: "True behaviour change is identity change. You might start a habit because of motivation, but the only reason you'll stick with one is that it becomes part of your identity."

If you have any further questions, I would be happy to respond personally: ap@agustin peralt.es.

Your opinion counts.
We shall be glad to include your comments on this book in future editions.
Please let us know what you think on our website:
www.plataformaeditorial.com

Please ask your usual bookseller about our titles.

"I cannot live without books."
THOMAS JEFFERSON

Plataforma Editorial plants a tree
for each title that it publishes.